645 Pap

Paper, Heather J.

Knack green decorating &
  remodeling : design ideas
  and sources for a

BC

$19.95
ocn213601910
12/16/2008

KNACK™
MAKE IT EASY

GREEN DECORATING
& REMODELING

KNACK™

GREEN DECORATING
& REMODELING

Design Ideas and Sources for a Beautiful
Eco-Friendly Home

HEATHER PAPER

KNACK™
MAKE IT EASY

Guilford, Connecticut
An imprint of The Globe Pequot Press

Text Design by Paul Beatrice

Cover photo credits:
Front Cover (left to right): Courtesy of Garnet Hill, Courtesy of VivaTerra, Courtesy of VivaTerra, Courtesy of BranchHome.com
Back Cover: Courtesy of Gaiam

Library of Congress Cataloging-in-Publication Data

Paper, Heather J.
   Knack green decorating & remodeling : design ideas and sources for a beautiful eco-friendly home / Heather Paper.
      p. cm.
   ISBN 978-1-59921-377-4
   1.   House furnishings. 2.   Green products. 3.   Dwellings--Remodeling.   I. Title. II. Title: Knack green decorating and remodeling.
   TX311.P27 2008
   645--dc22
                               2008012808

The following manufacturers/names appearing in *Green Decorating & Remodeling* are trademarks:
FLOR™, Greenguard™, Insuladd®, Eco-Cem®, Paperstone™, Syndecrete™, Green Seal®, Veriflora™, Eco Tex™

Printed in China
10 9 8 7 6 5 4 3 2 1

To my husband Russ, for your endless love and support

Acknowledgments

The preparation for writing this book started with my going to school, in a manner of speaking. Working in Seattle for a number of months gave me a broad education in eco-friendly design. For that opportunity, and others, I have to thank Matthew Dakotah, who is both a mentor and friend. My thanks, too, go out to some of that city's most forward-thinking designers and architects. Their creativity continues to inspire me in my own greener lifestyle.

CONTENTS

INTRODUCTION

Like most people, I've noticed the increasing ground-swell of green thinking over the past few years. But while working in Seattle a few years ago, my eyes were opened to the vast number of eco-friendly options. The magazine I was working on at the time had long since established an annual green issue, not done as of yet by any of the Midwest and Southeast publications I'd worked for. In Seattle I found designers and architects specializing in environmentally-conscientious projects and retailers devoted to green products. City programs were—and still are—designed to encourage eco-friendly practices. In short, green seemed to be at the forefront of everyone's minds.

That said, I never felt any pressure to be 100 percent green—that my home had to be environmentally friendly and the car I drove needed to be a hybrid and the food I ate had to be organic. Instead I quickly learned that, while eco-friendly possibilities were everywhere, it came down to a personal decision; you can be just as green as you want to be. A person might opt to simply replace the standard light bulbs in his or her home with compact fluorescents (which last ten times longer and use 75 percent less energy) or go green all the way.

It makes sense, too; going green is a process, a constant evolution. And it's the premise of this book. In the pages ahead, you'll find a wide variety of environmentally friendly decorating and remodeling ideas. Some are more green than others; an item designed with durability in mind (and, thus, long-term use) is green in its own right, but a durable item made of sustainable or recycled materials is even more so.

So, as you peruse these pages, keep in mind that goods can qualify as being green in several ways.

Renewable or sustainable materials

A renewable resource is one that is capable of being replenished, either by reproducing itself or through another natural process; as a general rule, the process takes no more than a few decades. Bamboo is a prime example of a readily renewable resource, because the fast-growing grass can be ready to harvest after just three to four years.

Sustainable materials, on the other hand, refer to those that are used or harvested in such a way that they don't deplete or permanently damage the material in question, meeting present-day needs without compromising the needs of future generations.

Furnishings or building materials made with managed-growth wood

Sustainable forest management standards have been put in place for the long-term health of forest ecosystems. Products that have the Forest Stewardship Council (FSC) seal, for instance, certify that the wood has come from forests managed in an environmentally and socially

responsible way. Hardwoods, softwoods, veneers, and even particleboard can have the FSC seal of approval. That includes many of today's engineered woods, too; the thin veneer top layer, as well as the substrate, is just as likely to be produced in a responsible way.

In addition to the FSC, organizations that adhere to sustainable forest-management standards include the American Tree Farm System (ATFS), Canada Standards Association (CSA), Maine Master Logger Certification, and the Sustainable Forestry Initiative (SFI).

Products that are durable, designed for long-term use

Perhaps you like to cook with a cast-iron skillet. Or maybe your bathroom walls are covered with glass tile. The two materials may seem to have nothing in common but, in fact, they do have a shared point of view. Both are durable, meaning that they'll last for years—and keeping them out of the landfill that much longer.

Even better, many durable items can ultimately be recycled in one way or another. That cast-iron skillet might be handed down to the next generation, while the glass wall covering could be melted down to create entirely new tiles.

Items made within 500 miles of the store you purchase them in

The concept is simple, if you think about it: By purchasing furniture and/or building products locally, you not only avoid shipping costs but also minimize the transportation distance, which in turn greatly reduces that product's embodied energy. And, if the item in question is locally made, so much the better; it will help support your local economy, too.

Products that have been recycled or reclaimed

Recycled materials are those that would otherwise be designated as waste, but have been remanufactured to create an entirely new product. The chair that your mother rocked you in as a baby might be passed on to your own daughter someday. Or too-small clothing might be cut into squares and incorporated into a new quilt.

Reclaimed materials, on the other hand, are those that have been used before and can been re-used without any reprocessing. They're often adapted in some way—perhaps cut to a different size or refinished—but basically retain their original form. Lengths of wood once used for bleachers, for instance, might be used to create wall paneling with vintage character.

Nontoxic fabrics and finishes

When shopping for green products, beware of what you can't see. Paints, stains, and glues often have volatile organic compounds (VOCs) that can affect internal air quality and give off potentially harmful vapors.

Instead, look for products that are less toxic or completely nontoxic; low- and no-VOC paints, for instance, are clearly labeled as such on the can. Likewise, opt for fabrics made of natural fibers or, even better, those that are organic. And be sure that any upholstery that is treated for fire resistance, waterproofing, and/or stain-proofing is nontoxic, too.

Products that minimize energy consumption

Some products that fall into this category are obvious. Well-insulated windows can go a long way in making your home energy efficient, not to mention well-placed ones that allow a tile floor, for instance, to soak up solar energy. And tight-fitting exterior doors are a natural to keep drafts out and a home's warm or cool air in.

Energy-efficient products can run the gamut, though, from Energy Star–rated appliances to the smallest compact fluorescent bulb. Think beyond consumer goods to eco-friendly methods, too. On a warm day, forgo the clothes dryer and hang your laundry outdoors, instead.

Organic products

In order to be classified as organic, products must be grown, raised, or dyed without the use of synthetic chemicals, heavy metals, or GMOs (genetically modified organisms). Additionally, they must be biodegradable and free of toxins and irritants. Organic cotton, for instance, must meet a set of strict National Organic Program (NOP) standards.

Because these standards require a three-year conversion for land before organic crops can be harvested, becoming an organic cotton producer is a long-term investment. As a result, organic cotton is more expensive than its conventional counterpart, but it's worth the green peace of mind.

Handcrafted items

Items that are handcrafted may not be the first thing you think of in terms of green products. But consider just how much energy is saved in terms of manufacturing, from prepping the components right through to the finishing process. Conveyor belts alone required for mass-produced pieces take an enormous amount of energy, not to mention the various other machines.

Because handcrafted items get personal attention, they're often superior in construction, too. What's more, it's easier to control potentially green aspects such as fabric, paint, and glue when a particular piece is handmade.

Fair-Trade practices

In a fair-trade system, workers receive living wages and employment opportunities for the goods they produce. You may, for instance, have had a fair-trade cup of coffee this morning and didn't even realize it. International organizations help workers market and sell goods—including crafts and agricultural products—for which they receive a stable, minimum price.

Want to know if a particular product is fair trade or not? Goods can be officially certified as fair trade by groups such as the Fair Trade Labelling Organization (FLO).

Given these green concepts, take a look at the chapters ahead. You'll probably discover that you're already more green that you thought you were—but not as much as you ultimately want to be, either. And, while you'll rarely find products that meet all, or even most, of the criteria above, the number of decorating and remodeling products with green attributes continues to grow every day.

Because the green industry is such a hot issue, it continues to change and grow daily. So use this book as it's intended—as a guide to your own greener lifestyle. Once you've poured over a chapter of particular interest, go to the back of the book to find a list of resources that can give you more information and prod-

uct ideas. We've even provided a basic glossary of terms to help you differeniate among various green goods.

This book has made me more passionate about creating a more eco-friendly home. Here's hoping it does the same for you.

THE LIVING ROOM

Make your living space more green and eco-friendly by transforming it gradually over time.

In the living room, there are plenty of eco-friendly options. It's simply up to you how many, or how few, green goods you choose to incorporate. Doing something as simple as changing a light bulb, for instance, can be a substantial step toward going green. But why stop there? Many of today's earth-friendly upholstery fabrics are just as fashion-forward as the alternative. And flooring, for that matter, provides a wide range of possibilities—from hard surfaces made of sustainable materials to soft rugs created from recycled plastic. Everything, right down to the accessories, can be green in one way or another. To express your personal style, think outside the box. If you're a bicycle enthusiast, what better

First Steps: Change a Light Bulb

- A compact fluorescent CFL bulb used in place of a standard incandescent costs a bit more but will last ten times longer than its conventional counterpart.

- CFLs use approximately 75 percent less electricity and have fewer carbon dioxide emissions.

- CFLs produce about 75 percent less heat, too, which cuts down on home cooling costs.

- Standard CFLs can be used in table and floor lamps as well as sconces and pendants and any open fixture that allows airflow.

Gradual Changes: Add Earth-friendly Upholstery

- Upholstery fabrics that are considered eco-friendly include natural materials such as cotton, hemp, and silk.

- Some of the more unusual alternatives are those made of bamboo, cork, and even corn.

- Fabrics made out of recycled materials, such as plastic soda bottles, are also green.

- Look for furniture that not only has eco-friendly upholstery, but is green right down to the frame and filling.

way to flaunt your style than to have a table made of bike parts! Be forewarned, though, that many of today's offerings are so smart looking, so cutting-edge, that you'll be tempted to go to the extreme.

Meanwhile, many concepts that are good for Mother Earth are healthier alternatives, too. That same table made of bicycle parts keeps hardware from hitting the landfill, but the benefits of something like nontoxic paint are twofold; not only does it keep poisonous fumes out of the air, it keeps them out of your circulatory system, too.

GREEN ● LIGHT

When in search of green products, don't overlook the durability factor. If something is particularly sturdy or can be easily repaired, there's less likelihood that it will end up in the landfill. Plus, a durable item is more cost effective. Even if the initial cost is a little more than you'd usually spend, its longevity will save you money in the long run.

Decorating Dictums: Use Bamboo Underfoot

- As an eco-friendly alternative to conventional hardwood, bamboo (a grass) grows fast and is ready for harvest after just three to four years.

- Bamboo is available in conventional planks, like hardwood, comprised of laminated strips of bamboo.

- Like wood, bamboo comes in various grades, differentiating hardness and quality. Typically, though, bamboo is harder than red oak.

- Bamboo flooring ranges in color from very light to dark brown shades.

Novel Ideas: Recycle a Bicycle

- Recycling old items, from bikes to bed frames, can be an inexpensive and innovative way to go green.

- The recycled wheel rims and gears in tables like the one above are never put together the same way twice, so each piece is unique.

- The glass top is easy to clean and can be recycled in the future.

- This kind of versatile table can be "recycled" from room to room, too.

THE HOME OFFICE

Even the most high-tech space can be an integral part of a green lifestyle.

With today's proliferation of computers, printers, and other electronics, the home office has the potential to be the least eco-friendly room in the house. With just a few changes, though, whether it's the purchase of an Energy Star–approved computer or your commitment to recycle all paper goods, the office can be as green as any other room.

The first step couldn't be simpler: Completely turn off the computer when it's not in use. Sure, it's tempting to let it lull into sleep mode; you can resume work, when you're ready, that much faster. But isn't it worth a few seconds of your time to save precious energy? For that matter, take a good, hard look at the amount of paper you generate. Think twice

First Steps: Turn Off the Computer

- While it's more time-effective to log off a computer so you can quickly resume working, turning it off is a more energy-efficient option.

- Alternatively, enable the computer's "power save" function, which can reduce power consumption by more than half when it's not being used.

- "Smart" power strips, available in office supply stores, eliminate idle currents, adding up to 10 percent energy savings.

- Even if turned off completely, appliances use energy when they're plugged in. Unplug the computer if you'll be gone for a few days.

Gradual Changes: Use Recycled Paper

- Recycling paper is a good idea; using recycled paper is even better.

- Using recycled paper helps slow the depletion of precious forestry resources.

- Recycled paper products also reduce the consumption of energy and, in turn, lessen the effect of global warming.

- To take sustainability to the next step, look for papers from Green-e certified mills.

about printing hard copies of emails and try to file more documents electronically, instead. While working toward the goal of a paperless office, though, opt for recycled paper.

Make smart decisions, too, about office furniture, whether you're looking for a recycled chair (there are great bargains to be found at used office supply stores) or new storage units (pieces made of sustainable materials are more prevalent than ever). In short, look in all the usual places for green products, and some of the more unusual, too.

Decorating Dictums: Add Eco-friendly Storage

- Look for furniture made of woods from well-managed sources, including those endorsed by the Forest Stewardship Council (FSC).

- Opt for furniture made locally, cutting down on energy needed to transport it—and cutting down on your costs, too.

- Consider furnishings made of recycled or reclaimed wood.

- If you want furniture that's green to the core, be sure it's not only made with sustainable materials but also made in an environmentally responsible way.

Novel Ideas: Use Reclaimed Wood

- Opt for a more uncommon covering for your walls and ceiling, such as reclaimed wood.

- One type of wood that is often reclaimed is Douglas fir, which is durable by nature.

- Some pieces are actually reclaimed bleachers from old gymnasiums, complete with their original stenciled seat numbers.

- Old bleachers are well-suited for other applications, too, including trim and wide-plank flooring.

THE KITCHEN

In a green kitchen, eco-friendly appliances are just the tip of the iceberg.

Start thinking about a green kitchen and you probably conjure up images of energy-saving appliances. Keep in mind, though, that there are smaller steps you can take on your way to a more eco-friendly space, many of which are less expensive than a new stove or dishwasher and others that need not cost a single cent.

Recycling is a prime example. Once you get in the habit of sorting recyclables, it soon becomes second nature. And by dedicating a space in the kitchen, it couldn't be more convenient. Keep recycling at the forefront of your thinking when choosing dinnerware and serve ware, too. You might be surprised at the mouthwatering colors of plates made

GREEN DECORATING & REMODELING

First Steps: Sort and Recycle

- Set up a recycling center in the kitchen, where most recyclables originate.

- Recycling centers can be freestanding, tucked into a corner of a pantry, or built into kitchen cabinetry.

- Some freestanding systems come on rolling racks, making them easier to move right out to the curb.

- An added benefit of an in-house system is that it reduces the need to open an exterior door each time you want to recycle, therefore saving energy, too.

Gradual Changes: Install Concrete Flooring

- Concrete floors are increasingly popular in the kitchen, largely due to how easy they are to maintain.

- Today's concrete can be stained, painted, or integrally colored to enhance any décor.

- If you're looking for more warmth underfoot, combine concrete with radiant heat.

- Concrete leaves your options open for the future, too; other floorings, such as hardwood, can be installed right on top of it.

of recycled glass. Likewise, it's not unusual to find serving trays crafted of reclaimed wood or even retired road signs in sturdy aluminum.

On a larger scale, look for flooring that's durable and furnishings made of wood from well-managed forests, like those that are FSC certified. You can identify these pieces by their Chain of Custody certificates, which track the wood used all the way back to its forest of origin. Taken one step at a time, the greening of your kitchen can happen at your own pace, one that suits your bottom line.

Decorating Dictums: Choose Green Chairs

- When it comes to kitchen seating, it's just as easy to be green as not; earth-friendly options are available in virtually every style.

- Look for chairs made of wood from well-managed forests, as well as other natural materials.

- Also consider seating made of recycled or reclaimed goods, such as aluminum, wood, and even plastic soda bottles.

- For very green chairs, look for those made with nontoxic glues and low- or no-VOC (volatile organic compound) paints.

Novel Ideas: Look for a Sign

- When it comes to serving trays, think outside the box. Recycled road signs, for instance, are sturdy and real attention getters.

- These hand-formed aluminum pieces are easy to clean.

- Storage is simple, too; a small hole drilled in each allows them to be displayed prominently on the wall.

- No two pieces are alike, making each a unique work of art.

THE BEDROOM

By going beyond eco-friendly bed linens, you'll soon be sleeping easier in your green retreat.

Consider the well-dressed bed to be a model for the ultimate eco-friendly sleeping spot. Every layer, from the box springs to the comforter, has the potential to be green. Adapt that layered principle to the rest of the room, and you'll have a space that's eco-friendly from floor to ceiling.

The walls that surround your space, for instance, might be coated with no-VOC paint. Or, consider Venetian plaster. Unless you're experienced with decorative wall finishes, though, let a pro apply your Venetian plaster. If you choose to do it yourself, be aware that not all Venetian plasters are all natural. Smart choices for such large expanses can go a long way in upping your green quotient, so why not make the same move with

First Steps: Switch to Organic Sheets

Gradual Changes: Plaster the Walls

- Natural cotton sheets are good, organic cotton even better. Organic cotton is grown using methods that have less of an impact on the environment.

- Organically produced cotton reduces the need for fertilizers and pesticides.

- Natural fibers like cotton promote better sleep by absorbing moisture better than their polyester counterparts.

- Organic cotton is a healthy alternative, too, because it's hypoallergenic.

- Add color and texture to bedroom walls with a covering of Venetian or "Italian" plaster, a thin veneer of lime mixed with marble, quartz, or clay.

- To create a serene atmosphere, color the plaster with a soothing hue.

- True Venetian plaster doesn't require any kind of wax or sealer, though these finishes are sometimes used for embellishment purposes.

- One of Venetian plaster's most eco-friendly aspects is its durability.

your flooring, too? Sustainable bamboo topped with natural wool rugs can create a cozy atmosphere, but there's no need to completely rule out wall-to-wall carpet. More major carpet manufacturers are taking a green approach to their products. You'll find low-VOC carpet tiles, too, that are easy to install.

The layers wouldn't be complete, though, without furnishings that have a green attitude. Buy pieces made of sustainable materials, preferably that use nontoxic paint and adhesives. Recycle by using an heirloom dresser. Incorporate items that can be used later in another way—or in another room.

Decorating Dictums: Put Down Carpet Tiles

- For an eco-friendly alternative to wall-to-wall carpet, try modular tiles. Many are made of hemp or wool with backings that contain recycled materials.

- Carpet tiles, like those sold by FLOR, have fewer VOCs than some broadloom carpets.

- Due to their modular nature, carpet tiles can be mixed and matched to create any size rug or a wall-to-wall look.

- The tile approach also allows a single piece to be replaced, if necessary, prolonging the life of the overall flooring.

Novel Ideas: Add Style with a Twist

- Using multipurpose furnishings is one of the best ways to be green. A stool like this, for instance, can also serve as a side table or simply a sculptural work of art.

- This piece is hand turned, showing off the wood's natural beauty to its best advantage.

- Because the mango wood is unfinished, there are no harmful toxins to worry about.

- The unfinished surface requires less care, too— just an occasional feather dusting.

THE BATHROOM

Tubs and toilets aren't the only candidates for replacement when creating a more eco-friendly bath.

A bathroom can be virtually bathed in green. From low-flow showerheads to thick bamboo towels to hardware made of recycled materials, there are opportunities at every turn. What's more, most are do-it-yourself projects, allowing you to be more efficient with your decorating/remodeling budget, too.

Saving water is a top priority, something you can do without spending a dime. It's nothing short of astounding, for instance, how much water you'll save by simply turning off the faucet while brushing your teeth. Replace the faucet itself with a low-flow model and you can make even more of a difference.

First Steps: Turn Off the Water

- You'll save 4 gallons of water per brushing by turning off the water while brushing your teeth.

- For a family of four, that equates to approximately 800 gallons per month.

- Turn off the water while shaving to save another 400 gallons per month.

- Immediately repair leaky faucets; they're perhaps the single-worst culprit of wasted water.

Gradual Changes: Add a Low-Flow Toilet

- Low-flow toilets are now mandatory. The National Policy Energy Act mandates toilets use no more than 1.6 gallons per flush.

- Replacing a conventional toilet with a low-flow model can save nearly 2,000 gallons of water per month.

- There are different types of low-flow toilets. Some feature redesigned bowls and tanks for better flushing while others are fitted with vacuum pumps.

- Most low-flow fixtures don't require any special fittings, making them easy to install.

A growing number of people are opting for bathrooms with no water-guzzling tub at all. But the bathroom is about more than plumbing products. In fact, there's nary an item that can't be green, right down to the all-natural soap. If you prefer metal knobs and pulls, look for those made of recycled metals. On the other hand, if you want something more colorful, consider those made of recycled glass. Likewise, you'll find towels made of sustainable bamboo and rugs made of eco-friendly cotton—some even crafted from old T-shirts.

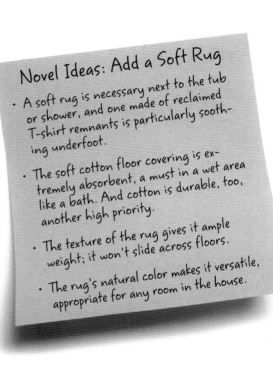

ZOOM

Low-flow faucet aerators and showerheads are available in a variety of different styles. Not only are these options better for the environment; the cost for these more eco-friendly options is little more than their conventional counterparts.

Decorating Dictums: Replace Pulls and Knobs

- To add personal style as well as a touch of green, replace worse-for-the-wear or dated pulls and knobs with new ones made of recycled materials.

- Recycled glass is one of the best options, offering a wide variety of shapes and colors.

- Glass is easy to maintain, requiring nothing more than a quick wipe down.

- Hardware made of recycled glass can be recycled again in the future.

Novel Ideas: Add a Soft Rug

- A soft rug is necessary next to the tub or shower, and one made of reclaimed T-shirt remnants is particularly soothing underfoot.

- The soft cotton floor covering is extremely absorbent, a must in a wet area like a bath. And cotton is durable, too, another high priority.

- The texture of the rug gives it ample weight; it won't slide across floors.

- The rug's natural color makes it versatile, appropriate for any room in the house.

THE LAUNDRY ROOM

Wash your clothes in an eco-friendly way for less wear and tear on the environment.

How often do you throw clothes into the laundry, with nary a thought as to how it affects the environment? The right detergent, the right appliances, and even the way you wash and dry makes a difference. You'll save gallons of water, for instance, by carefully matching the washer's water level with the load going in. By making some good choices in the laundry room, you can make a difference for the earth, too.

By simply switching to an eco-friendly detergent you can immediately rid the water and your clothes of toxic chemicals. A laundry sorter may seem less important, but it has green benefits, too. You can see at a glance when you have a full load, which is the most efficient way to do laundry.

First Steps: Use an Eco-Friendly Detergent

- When choosing a laundry detergent, keep it simple; fragrances, dyes, and brighteners don't make clothes any cleaner.

- Added chemicals may also trigger allergies or asthma. Read labels carefully, looking more for what's not in the formula than what is.

Use a powder detergent instead of liquid; you will use much less precious water (the primary ingredient of liquids).

Gradual Changes: Buy an Energy-Efficient Washer

- A conventional washing machine uses approximately 40 gallons of water per load; a more efficient model can cut energy costs by up to 70 percent.

- Savings come not only in electricity used, but also water and the energy needed to heat the water.

- Front-loading machines can cut water consumption by up to 40 percent.

- Some studies show that energy-efficient models actually clean clothes better.

An energy-efficient washer, meanwhile, offers eco-friendly benefits that are threefold: You save water, the energy needed to heat it, and electricity costs, too. Steam-cleaning washers for the home are now available, too. These machines reduce shrinkage and, thus, make your clothes last longer while using 35 percent less water and less energy, too. The downside, however, is that a single cycle can take more than two hours, which increases electrical use. Still, it's good to consider all of today's laundry options, even the most energy-efficient dryer—the clothesline.

ZOOM

When shopping for a new washing machine, consider ENERGY STAR models. The logo appears on the appliances that are the most energy efficient in their class. Manufacturers and retailers are allowed to put ENERGY STAR labels on those appliances that either meet or exceed standards set by the U.S. Environmental Protection Agency and the U.S. Department of Energy.

Decorating Dictums: Sort Out Some Style

- Choose and use a laundry sorter made of a sustainable material such as sea grass.

- Sorting as you go lets you know when you have a full load of laundry, making the washing process more efficient.

- Natural cotton bags within the laundry sorter can be washed as easily as the clothes themselves.

- Casters make it simple to roll the sorter from room to room on wash day.

Novel Ideas: Line Up

- When it comes to drying clothes, take the simple approach—hang them out on the line.

- Line drying clothes not only saves electricity but also prevents extraneous carbon dioxide from entering the atmosphere.

- Sunlight is a natural bleaching agent and disinfectant.

- Wipe the line clean on a regular basis, so freshly washed clothes don't get soiled right away.

TABLES
Like any other piece of furniture, a table can be green in more ways than one.

A table built to withstand the test of time can be passed from generation to generation, which fulfills one of the most basic green concepts—that of recycling. While you're at it, though, why not take your eco-friendly action one step further and purchase a table made of environmentally sound materials? If you think that will limit your style options, you're in for a pleasant surprise; you'll find that, in truth, it does anything but.

Wood is naturally the first material that comes to mind, but not all wood tables are created equal. Your best bet is to choose one that can be traced back to a responsibly managed forest, like those that are Forest Stewardship Council

Wood

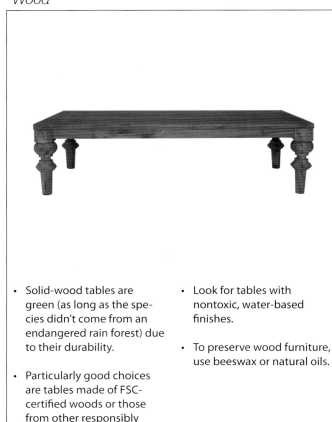

- Solid-wood tables are green (as long as the species didn't come from an endangered rain forest) due to their durability.

- Particularly good choices are tables made of FSC-certified woods or those from other responsibly managed forests.

- Look for tables with nontoxic, water-based finishes.

- To preserve wood furniture, use beeswax or natural oils.

Bamboo

- One of the best sustainable resources, bamboo, a species of grass, grows approximately five times faster than most hardwoods.

- Bamboo is durable, too; it's stronger than both red oak and maple.

- This natural material needs no replanting and flourishes without fertilizers or pesticides.

- Look for bamboo furnishings made with nontoxic adhesives and eco-friendly finishes.

(FSC)–certified. Laminated tables and plywood pieces can also be considered green, as long as they're bonded with nontoxic, formaldehyde-free adhesives. Or go another route with a table made of sustainable bamboo, an option that offers the same kind of durability or even more.

Metal tables have their advantages, too, especially in terms of durability. What's more, metal can eventually be melted down, to be used again in some other form. Most surprisingly, though, are the various—and vast—types of tables that are made of reclaimed and recycled materials.

Metal

- While metal isn't a sustainable material, tables made out of it are durable, making them good candidates for recycling in the future.

- Metal tables can be recycled in their original state or melted down to create something new.

- Some of today's recycled metal tables are completely unrecognizable from their original form, such as aluminum cans.

- To add a touch of warmth to a metal table, look for one that combines metal and wood or metal and bamboo.

Recycled Materials

- When shopping for tables, look for styles that are made of recycled materials and/or can be recycled once you're through with them.

- By utilizing recycled items, you conserve natural resources and reduce energy costs.

- Some of today's recycled tables include those made of recycled plastic jugs, reclaimed barn wood, recycled paper, and cardboard.

- Part of the beauty of recycled pieces is their provenance; the aged look is part of the charm.

SEATING
Practically any material can be transformed into a chair, upping the design possibilities considerably.

The days when all chairs were made of sturdy wood are gone. Today, you're just as likely to find seating pieces made of anything that will support a person. This is particularly good news for the green movement; innovative approaches to common materials and novel uses of those not so common are providing more options than ever before.

Like tables, chairs are commonly made of sturdy, solid wood. And, while you'll find them in traditional styles, you'll find them in not-so-traditional ones, too. Independent furniture designers, in particular, are adept at giving tried-and-true forms a new twist. Even the types of wood being used run the gamut more than ever; exotic species such as cork

Solid Wood

- Solid woods such as maple, oak, birch, and ash are good options for sturdy seating pieces.

- Their solid aspect makes them last a long time; fewer replacements equate to a decreased need for more natural resources.

- Wood in its natural state can be maintained with natural products, such as beeswax and linseed oil.

- Make sure that painted wood pieces utilize low- or no-VOC (volatile organic compound) coverings.

Sustainable Materials

- Wood is, perhaps, the most sought-after sustainable material used in seating pieces.

- In addition to common hardwoods, there are more exotic species of trees that are suitable, including monkey pod and cork.

- While sustainable furnishings can be more costly than conventional pieces, their contribution to the green movement balances the equation.

- Other sustainable options include reclaimed materials, such as wrought iron.

and monkey pod are striking and sustainable, too. At the top of the sustainability ladder, though, is bamboo—one of several grass-like materials that adapts well to seating pieces. Water hyacinth is another natural alternative, but to make it more stable it's often wrapped around a base of rattan.

The next time you're riding in a car, take a look at the seatbelt you're wearing. Seatbelt straps are just one of the reclaimed and recycled materials used to create innovative seating. It makes perfect sense; if seatbelts are strong enough to protect you in a car, they're sturdy enough to sit on.

Sustainability is such a hot issue that recently the Sustainable Furniture Council has been formed. It includes both individual and corporate members. For more information, go to www .sustainablefurniturecouncil.com.

Bamboo

- The strength of bamboo makes it a natural for furniture construction.

- Bamboo is lightweight, too, making chairs easy to move from room to room.

- The pliability of bamboo allows it to be formed in a comfortable, ergonomic fashion.

- Bamboo, like wood, can be given a wide variety of finishes, such as cherry and ebony.

Recycled Materials

- Chairs made of recycled materials are plentiful, with recycled or reclaimed wood being one of the most popular options.

- Recycled aluminum, in brushed or polished finishes, is another good choice for recycled seating.

- Other recycled materials conducive to chair design include plastic bottles, seatbelts, even staves from old wine barrels.

- Old theater seats, too, can be transformed into modern-day chairs.

UPHOLSTERY

Today's upholstery choices allow you to go green in the fabric, frame, and filling.

It's one thing to buy an upholstered seating piece covered in an eco-friendly fabric. It's even better if you can find a sofa, lounge chair, or ottoman that's environmentally sound right down to the filling and frame. Fortunately, more and more manufacturers are following that path, providing an increasing number of style options in the process. As a result, each day it's getting easier to be green.

Upholstery fabrics made of natural fibers are still, by far, the most common, with cotton, linen, and wool at the head of the pack. They're easy to dye, giving them countless color possibilities, and "breathe" well, too. That means that, when you're sitting on a piece upholstered in a natural fiber, it's more com-

Natural Fabrics

- Cotton, linen, wool, and silk are the most common natural upholstery fabrics.

- In addition to natural upholstery, look for products with attributes such as FSC-certified wood frames, water-based wood finishes, and pillows with recycled-fiber filling.

- Some furniture-makers use products that eliminate chlorofluorocarbon (CFC) gases from their manufacturing components; CFCs are one of the main culprits in deteriorating the ozone layer.

Hemp

- Hemp is both versatile and durable, providing the same kind of warmth and softness as other natural fibers.

- The hollow fibers of hemp have natural insulation properties.

- The hemp plant is not only fast-growing; it leaves the soil in good condition for succeeding crops and requires few, if any, pesticides or sprays.

- Hemp upholstery is available in its natural hue but can also be dyed in a wide variety of shades.

fortable than, say, vinyl—which during hot weather you tend to stick to. Hemp, too, is more and more readily available, with the same warmth and softness as other natural fibers.

But if natural fibers are good, organic fibers are even better. Cotton and hemp are often grown organically, and, for that matter, wool can be organic, too, as long as it can be traced back to sheep that were raised in an organic way. To be called organic, however, products—and their producers— must pass a rather stiff certification process, an extra step that can make the product a bit pricier, too.

Organic Materials

- Cotton is perhaps most often thought of as being organic.

- Organic cotton can also take the form of patterns and prints; the durable fiber can even be woven into plain as well as jacquard and herringbone patterns. Low-impact inks and dyes are typically used to meet fiber-processing standards.

- Another organic option is hemp.

- Hemp and cotton are sometimes blended, creating an upholstery fabric that features the best attributes of both.

Eco-friendly Upholstery Cleaners

- Green upholstery cleaners are safer than their chemical-based counterparts for removing food and dirt from furniture.

- These liquids commonly contain vegetable-derived soaps.

- As a rule, these cleaning compounds are unscented, making them a good choice for people who suffer from allergies.

- The cost is comparable to conventional upholstery cleaners.

STORAGE
Green storage solutions are, to a great degree, limited only by your imagination.

Whether you're in search of a petite dresser or a grandiose chest, there are plenty of storage pieces to be found with eco-friendly options. What's more, style and sustainability are by no means mutually exclusive. Some of today's finest green options feature cutting-edge combinations of materials, intricate inlays, even highly decorative hardware.

Well-built pieces made of solid wood have durability going for them, not to mention the inherent warmth of the wood itself. If you doubt its longevity, take a look in a local antiques store; many of the oldest and finest pieces are made of solid, maple, cherry, walnut, and oak. Searching antiques stores has another advantage, too. Any treasures you take home are

Wood

- Because storage units have to carry their own weight, and then some, wood is a solidly reliable material.

- Look for furnishings made of sturdy species such as maple, cherry, walnut, and oak.

- If your storage piece has a veneer, make sure it's applied with nontoxic adhesives.

- To prolong the life of the furniture, maintain wood with natural oils or beeswax.

FSC-Certified Wood

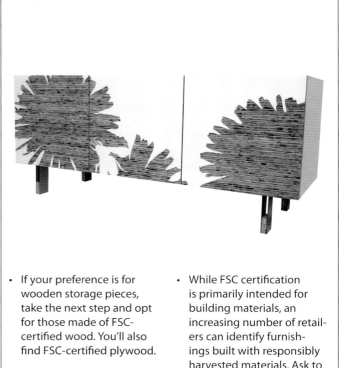

- If your preference is for wooden storage pieces, take the next step and opt for those made of FSC-certified wood. You'll also find FSC-certified plywood.

- FSC-certified forests support fair labor, protect ecosystems, and avoid the use of harmful chemicals.

- While FSC certification is primarily intended for building materials, an increasing number of retailers can identify furnishings built with responsibly harvested materials. Ask to see the Chain of Custody certificates.

being recycled, a concept at the very core of green living. For those who prefer new furniture, though, storage made of FSC certified wood is your assurance that it came from a responsibly managed source.

While bamboo storage pieces—and furniture in general, for that matter—used to be the exception, today they are closer to the rule. Its sustainability and durability make bamboo an attractive green option, while its caramel color adds a touch of warmth to any room. Likewise, reclaimed and recycled materials are being used to create innovative pieces.

Natural Materials

- Water hyacinth, in natural or dark tones, can be used to create lightweight but hardworking storage units.

- Other natural materials like bamboo, rattan, and banana fibers can also be utilized.

- If the natural fiber has a finish, be sure that it's formaldehyde free.

- Some furnishings made of natural materials can be used both indoors and out.

Recycled Materials

- Reclaimed wood is one of the sturdiest and most popular options for recycled storage.

- Recycled metal storage, made of materials like aluminum, is a good choice for kitchens, bathrooms, and mud rooms.

- Open-shelving units made of recyclable polypropylene come in bright colors as well as neutral hues.

- Layered cardboard pieces are recyclable, too; their honeycomb structure gives them durability.

BEDS

Sleep easier in a bed that's just as eco-friendly as it is fashion conscious.

You've heard it before: You spend at least one-third of your life in bed. So doesn't it make sense to take the time to find a sleeping spot that's well suited to your green lifestyle? No matter what your design preference may be, there's an eco-friendly option, one that's comfortable for you and your pocketbook, too.

From elaborate four-posters to simple platforms, the majority of beds are still made of wood. Those made of solid wood are not only sturdy, but can also be carved with intricate details. You'll sleep easier, though, if you choose one that features nontoxic paints and finishes. After all, you spend an average of eight hours a day in bed, and who

Wood

- Look for beds made of solid wood or, even better, wood from well-managed forests like those that are FSC certified.

- Any adhesives and finishes should be nontoxic so they don't offgas harsh fumes into the bedroom.

- The simpler in style your bed is, the less need there is for joints and glues, reducing the potential for toxic fumes, too.

- Likewise, opt for a headboard only and forgo the footboard.

Metal

- All metal beds are considered sustainable; their durability and resulting longevity make them green.

- You'll also find metal beds made of recycled content, taking the eco-friendly concept to the next level.

- Metal beds are available in headboard, headboard-and-footboard, and canopy styles, giving you a variety of options.

- Both metallic and painted finishes can be applied to metal beds, but look for those that are nontoxic.

wants to breathe in all those fumes? Metal beds are another good durable option but, as is the case with beds made of wood, beware of those that have less-than-earth-friendly paints and coatings.

Basically, the right bed for you comes down to a matter of priorities and personal style preference. An upholstered bed—wrapped in natural cotton, linen, wool, silk, or hemp—can add a splash of color and pattern to a room, while beds made of bamboo add natural warmth and speak to a commitment to sustainability.

MAKE IT EASY

When you're through with a piece of furniture, recycle it and hand it off to someone who can give it a new home, instead of sending it to the landfill. If that's not an option; contact the retailer/manufacturer you bought it from; they may be interested in taking it back to recycle some or all of the parts!

Upholstered

- Like seating, upholstered beds can have both green fabric as well as green filling and frames.

- There are a wide variety of styles, including headboard only, headboard-and-footboard, and platform.

- On some platform models, an upholstered "frame" softens the sides and the foot of the bed.

- Some upholstered pieces incorporate niches at the head of the bed, eliminating the need for bedside tables.

Bamboo

- Many of today's bamboo beds are barely recognizable as such; they look more like a light-colored wood than the grass substance they really are.

- Layered and pressed into planks, bamboo is an extremely strong material.

- Finishes on bamboo furnishings range from clear to a very dark chocolate brown.

- Bamboo furniture has gone mainstream; it's easy to find, even at discount retailers.

CABINETRY

Built-in cabinetry adds architectural interest and gives you the opportunity to go green from the ground up.

Cabinetry made of renewable resources without any toxic glues or finishes is advantageous to the environment and benefits chemically sensitive people, too. Traditionally, wood has been the overwhelming material of choice. And that really hasn't changed. If wood cabinets are your first choice, however, look for those with nontoxic paints and finishes.

But think beyond convention, too. Cabinets made of wheat board are eco-friendly. In addition wheat board gives many farmers a secondary income while processing the approximately sixty million tons of straw residue that becomes available each year. Fiberboard is another increasingly popular option. Made of recycled wood fibers, it costs considerably less

Wood

- All solid-wood cabinets are good choices; even better are those made of wood from responsibly harvested forests.

- Drawers and shelves should be equally green, if not made of solid wood, then made of materials such as formaldehyde-free plywood.

- Look for cabinetry made with nontoxic, water-based glues and finishes.

- To keep painted wood cabinetry green, use low- or no-VOC coatings.

Wheat Board

- As its name implies, wheat board is derived from a straw waste product.

- Bales of wheat straw are milled into fine particles, bound with a formaldehyde-free resin and then hot pressed into sheets of varying thickness.

- Wheat board is a relatively inexpensive option compared to cabinets made of solid wood.

- This type of cabinetry can be painted or stained like any other.

than solid-wood cabinetry. Because adhesives are a large part of its makeup, however, be sure that they're formaldehyde free. Bamboo is showing up in cabinetry, too—its strength and durability a good match for such a hardworking purpose. It has the added advantage of being biodegradable.

Considering the large percentage of space that cabinetry takes up in the average kitchen, this is one of the most important decisions you'll make. By making a smart choice—and a green one—you'll be taking a giant step forward for Mother Earth—and for yourself, too.

········· GREEN ● LIGHT ·············

When searching for cabinetry, think outside the box; cupboards don't necessarily have to be new. For instance, search out a local salvage store to find cabinetry to recycle in your own home. You may find solid-wood options or metal units that will suit your space.

FURNITURE

Fiberboard

- Cabinetry made of medium-density fiberboard is environmentally friendly because it's made of recycled wood fiber content.

- Cabinets made of fiberboard are less expensive than wood.

- Fiberboard is a sturdy alternative; at the same time, it's lightweight, making it easy to install.

- Formaldehyde-free fiberboard eliminates the possibility of offgassing, a process that can worsen when exposed to warmth—sunshine or hot appliances.

Bamboo

- Structurally sound and aesthetically appealing, bamboo is a good choice for cabinetry.

- Bamboo is not only sustainable, it's biodegradable, too.

- Cabinets made of bamboo come in a wide variety of styles, from traditional to sleek modern looks.

COTTON

When it comes to home furnishings fabrics, it's hard to beat cotton's down-to-earth qualities.

For home furnishings, natural fabrics are, well, a natural. And leading the way is "king" cotton. In either conventional or organic forms, its versatility makes it just as appropriate for lightweight, billowing curtains as it is for heavy-duty denim upholstery. It can take the form of casual gingham or more formal chintz. It can be anything you want it to be.

Conventional cotton is much more readily available than organic, but keep an eye on the kind of finish it has. Upholstery fabrics, for instance, often have stain-resistant finishes. While they're a great convenience, not all are nontoxic, so check the content. The same goes for cotton fabrics that have a glazed, or shiny, finish. In short, if the fabric has any

Upholstery

Bedding

- Cotton's resistance to wear, fading, and pilling makes it a good choice for upholstered furnishings.

- Certain weaves, such as duck and sailcloth, are more durable than others, such as damask.

- This fiber is less resistant to soil. Soil resistant finishes can be applied, but with them often come toxins, too.

- Because cotton takes color well, it's available in a wide variety of colors and patterns.

- Cotton is the most prevalent fiber used for bed linens, including sheets, pillowcases, duvet covers, and shams.

- Because this natural fiber breathes well, it's comfortable to sleep on.

- It's easy to care for, as well, though there can be some shrinkage after washing.

- Conventional cotton bedding is available in a wide variety of colors and patterns; organic cotton is more limited in its palette.

kind of surface treatment, investigate the contents carefully.

Likewise, look for fabrics with natural or at least nontoxic dyes. It's interesting to note, however, that not all cotton is naturally white. Limited amounts of cotton are being grown in shades of green, brown, red, and yellow. That means that the cotton needs minimal processing—and, specifically, no dying. Plus it doesn't fade like the chemically dyed variety. At this point, it's primarily limited to bed linens and baby clothes, but as its availability increases, the number of products will, too.

Window Treatments

- Cotton window treatments have good drapability, gathering easily into soft folds.

- Gingham is a good choice for casual curtains, while damask should be reserved for formal settings.

- Simple, unlined panels can sometimes be washed, but more complex designs usually require dry cleaning.

- If cotton curtains are lined, be sure that the lining is also made of cotton so the two materials wear at about the same pace.

Innovative Ways

- Natural cotton webbing creates a sturdy seating surface.

- The frame of this simple but classic design is crafted of maple, just as green as the basket-woven webbing itself.

- This particular chair is Greenguard certified, ensuring that—according to the Greenguard Environmental Institute (GEI)— chemical and particle emissions meet acceptable indoor air quality pollutant guidelines.

LINEN

Linen fabrics are luxurious, and (bonus!) they're eco-friendly, too.

Think of linen and you may recall your favorite summer shirt, the one that seems to wrinkle the minute you put it on. But that's just a part of its casual charm. Made from flax, linen can take myriad forms, woven into everything from sheer handkerchief linen to heavy canvas. Its natural luster makes it appealing and, because its staple is longer than cotton and other natural fibers, linen is often more durable, too. On the other hand, flax is more difficult to grow, so linen fabrics tend to be more expensive. In the right application, however, it's worth every cent.

Much of its beauty lies in the fact that flax is completely eco-friendly. Once the fiber's been extracted from the plant,

Upholstery

- Because linen upholstery fabrics soil and wrinkle easily, they're best reserved for formal living and dining rooms.

- This naturally strong fiber naturally resists pilling and fading, making it long lasting.

- Linen's natural color ranges from creamy white to beige to dark brown; this fiber takes color well, however, so it can be dyed to any hue.

- Linen upholstery must be professionally cleaned.

Bedding

- The natural softness of linen makes it one of the most luxurious types of bedding you can sleep on. The more linen bedding is washed, the softer and smoother it becomes.

- Because linen "breathes" well, it absorbs body moisture without feeling damp.

- Linen is relatively dust and stain resistant.

- Bedding made of 100 percent linen is more expensive than that made of cotton.

it's used to create clothing and home furnishings fabrics as well as paper. Even the paper currency we use is made of 75 percent cotton and 25 percent linen. Plus, flax oil is used to produce soap, cosmetics, even paint and printing inks. Not a single part of this plant is wasted.

In its natural state, linen fabrics range in color from cream to dark brown. Linen is at its strongest in its most basic form, too. Once it's chemically bleached or dyed, the fiber loses some of it's original strength, giving up some longevity at the same time.

FABRICS

Window Treatments

- Linen is a good choice for window treatments because it resists fading better than many other fibers.

- Linen offers a look of understated elegance in living and dining rooms.

- Although it doesn't gather into soft folds as easily as cotton, linen holds a sharp crease or pleat better.

- Linen window treatments, as a rule, must be professionally cleaned.

Innovative Ways

- Linen fabrics can be patterned, too. These pillows have been hand sprayed with dyes to give them the wood grain effect.

- The fabric's inherent texture adds to the pattern's appeal.

- Linen fabrics can also be patterned with stripes, florals, and intricate geometric forms.

- Removable pillow covers made of linen can often be machine washed and ironed.

WOOL

Wool can take on many guises, from filmy thin curtains to fuzzy thick blankets—and everything in between.

Not all wool is created equal. Worsted wools, such as gabardine, are made from longer fibers and have a more minimal nap. Woolens, on the other hand, such as flannel, are bulkier and have the soft, fuzzy surface most often equated with the fiber. And then, of course, there are special types of wool. Merino wool, for instance, from sheep of the same name, is regarded as the finest quality wool—and it doesn't itch, either. Each has its best end uses, depending on its weight and weave, but all are opulent in their own way.

The "greenest" form of wool is organic. To be labeled as such, however, there's a stringent set of standards. Pesticides can't be used on the pastures, and the sheep's feed must

Upholstery

- Some of the best wool-upholstery options include flannel and gabardine.

- Among wool's best attributes are that it's durable and comfortable; it's also resistant to pilling, fading, and soiling.

- Wool accepts dye easily. Thus, you can find the fiber in a virtual rainbow of colors.

- Wool-upholstered pieces typically require professional cleaning.

Bedding

- Wool bedding can take the form of wool-filled pillows and comforters, wool mattresses and pads, and, of course, blankets in a variety of weights.

- Like linen, wool absorbs moisture without feeling damp.

- Because wool is a natural insulator against both heat and cold, wool bedding is the perfect year-round choice.

- It naturally repels bacteria and dust mites—a plus for those with allergies or asthma.

be certified organic. The animals can't have been dipped in insecticides, and a limited number are allowed per acre, to prevent overgrazing. And—before any wool can be sold as organic—third-party certification is required to verify that all standards have been met. Largely due to the time it takes to bring farming practices up to organic values, this type of wool is in relatively short supply, making it more expensive than nonorganic varieties. As its availability continues to grow, look for organic wool in more and more types of home furnishings.

As a general rule, wool isn't cheap, but its durability and longevity makes it well worth the expense. To keep wool looking its very best, it generally needs to be professionally cleaned. Check the label, however; some items, such as blankets, are available in washable wool.

Window Treatments

- Because this fiber has some weight to it, wool is a good choice for window treatments. It drapes beautifully.

- Wool is a natural insulator, too, keeping out cold temperatures or the sun's too-warm rays.

- Wool doesn't deteriorate as quickly as most other fibers do when exposed to direct sunlight.

- This fiber is naturally flame resistant.

Innovative Ways

- Felted wool, made by condensing and pressing the fibers, results in a non-woven material, as in this seat cushion.

- Felt's nonwoven attribute means that the edges cannot ravel, making it more durable and long lasting.

- This type of wool can be purchased by the yard, just like any other fabric.

- Felt has the same soil-resistant and insulating properties found in any other wool fabric.

SILK

Even when used in the smallest amounts, silk adds an air of elegance to any interior.

Since it was discovered nearly 5,000 years ago in China, silk has been widely regarded as one of the most luxurious fibers. Due to its delicate nature, however, the use of silk in home fashions has to be considered carefully. It's perfectly suited for window treatments that you'll be admiring from afar, but it is not as appropriate for a sofa that's destined to get every-day wear and tear from kids and the family pet.

It's generally assumed that all silk worms have a diet of mulberry leaves. But wild silk is created when the silkworms eat oak leaves, instead. Shantung, Tussah, and Pongee silk all fall into this category. Silkworms are prolific producers, too; the average cocoon can contain one continuous thread up

GREEN DECORATING & REMODELING

Upholstery

- Silk in the form of a heavier weave, like brocade or damask, is appropriate for seating pieces in formal spaces, such as a living or dining room.

- Made from the cocoon of the silkworm, this natural fiber has a smooth texture and good resilience.

- Furniture upholstered in silk should be placed away from windows, because it can be susceptible to sun damage.

- Silk is expensive, as compared to other natural fibers, and must be professionally cleaned.

Bedding

- Habotai silk is often used for bed linens, including sheets and pillowcases. It has a very high thread count and is hypoallergenic.

- Lightweight tussah silk is another bedding option, good for duvet covers and shams. This wild silk has a linen-like texture.

- Silk-filled comforters are readily available, some wrapped in another layer of silk, others in cotton.

- Silk bedding is resistant to dust mites and mildew.

to 4,000 feet long. That may sound like a lot, but it takes approximately 2,500 silkworms to produce a single pound of raw silk.

Some silk threads are collected in a more sustainable way than others. Traditionally, the chrysalises are killed inside the cocoons, so as not to break the silk threads. In some instances, though, the fibers can be pulled from the cocoon after the moths have emerged. It's one more consideration when you're deciding how green you want to be.

Window Treatments

- Silk has excellent drapability, making it a good choice for window dressings.

- Dupioni silk, with slight variations in texture, is a good option, as is silk taffeta, characterized by a smooth, crisp hand.

- Due to the elegant nature of the fabric, silk draperies are generally formal in style.

- Because silk can deteriorate with prolonged exposure to the sun, window treatments made of this fabric must be lined and, sometimes, interlined.

Innovative Ways

- Silk, which can be dyed in a virtual rainbow of colors, can make an impact on a room in something as small as a decorative pillow.

- Taffeta and dupioni silk are good options; they can even be made to match window treatments.

- Because they don't get wear and tear, silk velvet is another option for pillows.

FABRICS

HEMP

Surprisingly similar to linen, hemp is a less-expensive but equally green option.

At first glance, hemp could be mistaken for linen; it has a similar appearance and even a similar hand. Like its counterpart, it wrinkles easily and adapts well to multiple uses. Unlike linen, though, hemp is purely an import, made from the stems of the cannabis sativa plant. It's important to note, however, that hemp fibers come from a very specific spe-

cies of cannabis, one with mere traces of the substance that makes its well-known counterpart (marijuana) a narcotic. Nonetheless, the plant that produces hemp fibers can't be grown in this country.

Still, many people seek out hemp for its eco-friendly aspects. Because it's such a hardy plant, it can be grown with-

Upholstery

- With its inherent warmth, hemp is a comfortable choice for upholstery.

- This fiber is durable, too, and will stand up to daily use.

- Because hemp readily accepts dye, the fabric comes in a variety of colors.

- Hemp blends well with other fabrics, such as cotton and silk, resulting in materials that have the best characteristics of each.

Bedding

- Sheets, pillowcases, and duvet covers are available in hemp, both organic and nonorganic varieties.

- Organic hemp, grown and processed without toxic chemicals, is hypoallergenic.

- Because hemp is a strong fiber, it's durable and long lasting.

- Hemp, which withstands water better than most other textiles, gets softer with every washing.

out the use of pesticides at all, which is why a lot of hemp is organic. Hemp can be used to produce everything from beauty products and fashion accessories to paper and pet supplies. Its durability translates to the finished fabric, as well, making it a good choice for upholstery and curtains. And even though the material is inherently coarse, it's often used for bed linens because it becomes softer with each repeated washing. In addition to being both versatile and green, it's an inexpensive option, too. It's no wonder that its popularity continues to grow.

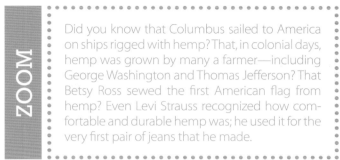
Window Treatments

- Hemp is resistant to UV rays, making it a good choice for residential window treatments.

- This fiber is a good insulator, too; hemp curtains can help shield out the summer sun and the winter cold.

- Hemp does not have the drapability of cotton or silk. It's better suited for flat-panel treatments.

- To keep the fibers from breaking down, hemp window treatments shouldn't be designed with sharp creases or pleats.

Innovative Ways

- A single element like the pillow above can take a minimal bite out of your budget and make maximum decorative impact.

- Part of the beauty of decorative pillows is their portability; they can be "recycled" from room to room.

- The softness of hemp translates well to decorative pillows.

- Hemp pillows filled with natural materials take green to the nth degree.

FABRICS

MORE BEAUTIFUL FABRICS

If you look around, you'll find green fabrics everywhere, even in the most unlikely places.

Natural materials such as cotton, linen, wool, silk, and hemp are just the tip of the iceberg in terms of eco-friendly fabrics. One of the most luxurious is cashmere, made from the hair of the Kashmir goat. Often used to make blankets, it's perfectly animal-friendly; to collect the hair, the goats are simply combed. Similarly, mohair—a popular choice for high-end upholstery—is made from the fleece of the Angora goat. In fact, mohair was often used to upholster the seats in early theaters and playhouses, chosen as much for its lush look as for its durability. Alpaca and bamboo are also being woven into throws, and even wood fibers and corn silk are being transformed into home furnishings fabrics.

Pillows

- Made of hand-woven raffia cloth by the Kuba people of the Congo, these pillows feature bold geometric patterns and rich textures.

- Use recycled fabrics—even old sweaters—to create your own one-of-a-kind decorative pillows.

- Flat-weave raffia cloth, made from raffia-palm leaves, can be left in its natural state or colored with organic red, brown, or ochre dyes.

- These Kuba pillows are backed with natural linen.

Throw

- Some throws are made from 100 percent corn silk, perhaps one of the least-known fiber sources.

- The texture of the fabric is much like soft cashmere.

- While this fiber is just as eco-friendly as its wool counterpart, this piece is less expensive than comparable cashmere would be.

- This throw provides a layer of warmth but isn't too heavy, either.

Additionally, any number of pieces can be recycled. A too-small T-shirt that you can't bear to part with can be turned into decorative pillows, as can old sweaters or a pair of jeans. Even recycled sailboat canvas is showing up in pillow forms. And that seatbelt you wear on a daily basis? The straps are now being woven into sturdy seating pieces. The possibilities are all around you; sometimes all it takes is a little creativity. And isn't that what creating personal style is all about?

Towels

- These towels are made of 100 percent beech wood. The wood is broken down into cellulose form, from which the microfiber is produced.

- Dyes used in the towels are nontoxic and colorfast.

- With a texture similar to that of cashmere, they are highly absorbent, easily wicking moisture away from the skin.

- Because they're lightweight, they dry faster and require less energy than conventional terry towels.

Innovative Ways

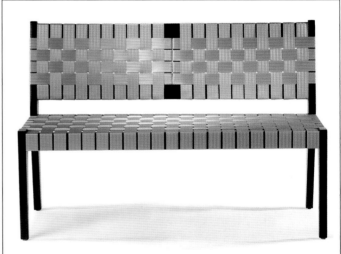

- Seatbelts are no longer only for safety purposes; this piece of furniture utilizes them for both the seat and back.

- The frame, made of solid maple, comes in a variety of colorful and natural stains.

- Standard black seatbelt webbing is available as well as other shades, including bright red and orange.

- Nontoxic water-based adhesives are used throughout, making this seating piece even more green.

FABRICS

35

PAINT

Just about every type of paint today is more eco-friendly than ever before.

When it comes to joining the green movement, the paint industry has made great strides; most major manufacturers now offer environmentally safe options in the form of low-VOC (volatile organic compound) and no-VOC paints. Because VOCs contain toxic substances, they can affect indoor air quality and even be hazardous to your health. Low- or no-VOC paints may cost a bit more, but they're well worth the peace of mind and personal health.

Those aren't the only green options; some companies offer recycled paint, too. Recycled paint can either be reprocessed or reblended. Reprocessed paint is a mix of recycled and new content, while reblended paint is simply remixed.

Low-VOC Paint

- Because these paints have fewer VOCs, there's less of a "new paint" odor.

- Low-VOC paints are available in nearly as many colors as conventional paints, and in similar finishes, too.

- Low-VOC paints, as well as no-VOC types, are particularly good choices for children's rooms.

- Even low- and no-VOC paints may have some toxins in their formulas, so read the label carefully.

No-VOC Paint

- No-VOC paints are available in flat, satin, and semigloss finishes, but colors are somewhat more limited than those found in conventional paint palettes.

- No paint can truly have "zero" VOCs, but less than five grams per liter (g/l) can be considered "zero" VOC.

- No-VOC primers are also available, which can add another layer of green to painted surfaces.

Although reblended coatings have a higher percentage of recycled paint, they're available in limited colors. For a list of recycled paint manufacturers, simply do an Internet search.

Whatever paint you use should always be stored properly for future use. If you don't think you'll use the leftover amount, "recycle" it by passing it on for someone else to use. Schools, churchs, and nonprofit organizations are often happy to accept it. But, if you've nowhere else to go, take leftover paint to your local recycling or household hazardous waste center.

●●●●●●●●●●● · GREEN ● LIGHT ·●●●●●●●●●●●●●●●

Look for paints that are Green Seal certified, based on their VOC content and the absence of chemicals, as well as durability, performance, and manufacturing practices. Green Seal is an independent, nonprofit organization that promotes environmentally responsible products and services. To learn more, go to www .greenseal.org.

Recycled Paint

- Recycled or reprocessed paint is typically sorted by type (interior vs. exterior), by light and dark colors, and by finish (high-gloss vs. flat). The recycled portion can range from 50 to 100 percent.

- Recycled paints are available in limited colors.

- Paint with recycled content is usually comparable in price to conventional paints, and you'll even find some that cost less.

- Several retailers offer recycled paints. They can be found at recycling centers, too.

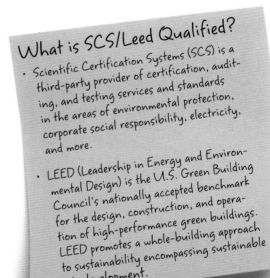

What is SCS/Leed Qualified?
- Scientific Certification Systems (SCS) is a third-party provider of certification, auditing, and testing services and standards in the areas of environmental protection, corporate social responsibility, electricity, and more.

- LEED (Leadership in Energy and Environmental Design) is the U.S. Green Building Council's nationally accepted benchmark for the design, construction, and operation of high-performance green buildings. LEED promotes a whole-building approach to sustainability encompassing sustainable site development.

PAINTS AND FINISHES

NATURAL PAINTS

Paints made of natural elements are a green choice that has been around for thousands of years.

Natural paints made entirely of raw materials offer not only good looks but also ease of mind because there are no health or environmental risks. Clay-based paints, for instance, are characterized by the soft glow of adobe. Because they are no-VOC coverings, clay paints are a good choice for kids' rooms or for those who have allergies. Though available in a more limited palette than conventional paint, this type of coating still covers a wide portion of the spectrum. Plus, you can buy the paint premixed in a can or purchase powdered pigments and make your own. Milk paints, on the other hand, come in powdered form only, so the consumer can choose how thick to make it—from a light wash to a

Clay

- Clay paints are available in a variety of soft tones and textures, effecting the look of clay plaster.

- Tints can be added to the basic subtle colors to create brighter hues.

- The natural mineral and plant-based components combine to create a washable matte finish.

- These paints can be used anywhere that conventional interior paints would be used.

Plant-Based

- Plant-based powders make good nontoxic paints but, because they're not washable, are best reserved for low-traffic areas.

- A no-VOC option, plant-based paint can be built up in layers to create a rich, textured finish.

- Clove oil can be added to plant-based paints, slowing the drying process of the oils and reducing the smell of turpentine.

- Because this type of paint doesn't stand up well to humidity, it shouldn't be used in kitchens or baths.

fully opaque paint. Milk paint has been around a long time, too; there's evidence of it on the walls of caves that date back six thousand years.

Likewise, plant-based powders can be used to create non-toxic wall coatings. This type of paint is best used in low-traffic areas, though, because it isn't washable. For that matter, keep in mind that any natural paint products may require special care in terms of surface preparation, application, and maintenance.

Milk Paints

- Milk paint, typically found in powder form, contains milk protein, lime, clay, and earth pigments to screate the various colors.

- This product replicates the homemade paint once made with skim milk or buttermilk, crushed limestone,

and pigments like those found around clay pits.

- Basic colors are limited but can be mixed to form various other hues.

- The dry powder can be hydrated to the thickness of a wash or a full-cover coat.

Whitewash

- True whitewash is a heavy-bodied opaque paint. Brush marks can be discernable in the finish.

- Whitewash is available in both smooth and fine-grit formulas.

- Whitewash is not only eco-friendly, it's economical, too.

- This covering can be used on unpainted or previously painted walls.

PAINTS AND FINISHES

SPECIALTY PAINTS

For those with specific needs or health issues, one of today's specialty paints may be the solution.

Those with strong sensitivities to chemicals—or anyone with asthma or allergies, for that matter—should take a look at today's wide variety of specialty paints. There's a type of paint for practically every specific purpose, and—with the increasing awareness of the environment—many of them are green. Low-biocide paints, for instance, don't have toxic additives such as fungicides and pesticides. Because those same additives are what give conventional paint its long shelf life, however, many low-biocide paints must be special ordered and used right away. Likewise, antimold paints don't have synthetic toxins or fungicides and their chlorine-free makeup has an antimold effect. Coated with this type of

Low-Biocide Paint

- Some biocides, such as pesticides, poisonous heavy metals, and other preservatives, can offgas just like VOCs.

- Low-biocide paints keep these chemicals to a minimum, making them a "healthier" option.

- These no-VOC, low-odor options inhibit the growth of stains and odors that can result in mold, mildew, and bacteria growth.

- Low-biocide paints are available in a limited number of colors.

Anti-Mold Paint

- Antimold paints contain no synthetic toxins and are free of fungicides.

- Because the formula is mineral based, it's eco-friendly.

- Available in a matte finish only, it can be applied to plaster or drywall.

- This type of paint is typically only available in white.

paint, even infested areas are resistant to reinfestation.

Solvent-free paints are generally void not only of solvents but essential oils and aromatic additives, too. And there are also odor-free paints, which have none of the typical "new paint" fumes. Like anything else, though, not all specialty paints are created equal. Do your homework to determine exactly what you do—and don't—want in a paint product. And know that, even with those paints that claim to be completely green, it's imperative to read the label to see what you're getting.

Solvent-Free Paint

- Solvent-free paints can be used as a base, tinted to almost any color; the tints themselves are also non-toxic.

- This type of paint is usually offered in both matte and satin finishes.

- It can be used on nearly any flat surface, including concrete and brick.

- Solvent-free paint also has no essential oils nor aromatic additives.

Odor-Free Paint

- Odor-free paints are available in a wide variety of colors and sheens.

- These paints are odor free just as soon as they're dry to the touch.

- Odor-free paints are available in eggshell, flat, and semigloss finishes.

- This type of paint comes as a white base, to which color can be added, or in a one-coat white that can be used alone.

PAINTS AND FINISHES

STAINS AND SEALERS

The highly toxic varnishes of yesterday have been replaced with plenty of green possibilities.

If you've gone to the trouble of finding eco-friendly wood for your home, be it in furnishings, walls, or flooring, the last thing you want to do is conceal the beautiful grain with opaque paint. Instead, look for wood stains and sealers that are equally green. For that matter, stains or sealers for any surface can be eco-friendly, too.

Like paints, wood stains can contain unhealthy levels of VOCs, biocides, and fungicides. (In fact, stains usually have more.) Still, it's important to protect wood from the sun's harmful UV rays. Nontoxic stains and sealants will do the job, albeit in a more earth-friendly way. Low-VOC sealers are also available; many are multipurpose and can be ap-

GREEN DECORATING & REMODELING

Wood Stain

- Wood stains that are SCS certified and LEED qualified are available for both interior and exterior surfaces.

- These stains have no aniline dyes, no aromatic solvents, and no formaldehyde.

- Look for semitransparent stains that allow the wood grain to shine through.

- Made of natural pigments and no dyes, these stains come in a variety of finishes, including cedar, walnut, birch, maple, redwood, mahogany, and oak.

Wood Sealer

- Natural wood sealers offer durable finishes for all wood, bamboo, and cork floors, including solid, parquet, and veneered surfaces.

- These sealers are free of biocides and preservatives and are made up of natural vegetable oils and waxes.

- Natural sealers are practically odorless during both application and while drying.

- This type of sealer is stain resistant to liquids, including spills of coffee, tea, soda, and milk.

plied to any porous product.

Sealants specifically made for stone surfaces are also available in nontoxic, water-based formulas. This type of sealant, which can be applied to everything from marble and granite to concrete and tile, can be clear—so the material keeps its natural look—or glossy. Either way, these sealers serve the functions of repelling water and preventing surfaces from staining. Consider them a small insurance investment.

Low-VOC Sealer

- Water-based, low-VOC sealers can be multipurpose, good for any porous product from wood to concrete.

- These products can reduce toxic outgassing, sealing in toxic formaldehyde found in processed wood.

- Their water base makes these sealers odorless once dry.

- Look for SCS-certified and LEED-qualified products.

Tile, Stone, and Masonry Sealer

- Clear, water-based sealers keep tile and masonry looking natural.

- The multipurpose sealers can be used on concrete, tile, stone, and even grout.

- Water-based sealers can provide stain protection as well as oil and water repellency.

- There are also water-based sealers that add a glossy sheen and color enhancement to tile, stone, and masonry.

FLOOR AND FURNITURE FINISHES

Breathe easier by finishing your floors and furniture with environmentally friendly products.

When it comes to furniture and floor finishes, it seems everything old is new again. Many of the same products that our grandparents used faithfully are the same ones that we're reaching for today.

Linseed oil, extracted from flax seed, has long been used as a preservative for wood. Raw linseed oil is very slow drying (depending on the size of the surface, it can take days or even weeks), so it's not the best option for floors and furniture. Boiled linseed dries more quickly, but it contains solvents. The most eco-friendly option is linseed oil that is polymerized, the natural process the oil goes through as it's transformed from a liquid to a solid. The resulting clear

Linseed Oil

- Naturally yellow in color, linseed oil produces a finish that seeps into the pores of the wood, forming a thin, soft film on the surface.

- The oil provides minimal protection against scratching, scuffing, staining, water, and water vapor.

- Linseed oil is easy to apply and yields a beautiful hand-rubbed look.

- This finish is best suited for furnishings that aren't subjected to excessive wear and tear.

Natural Oil

- Natural oils comprise ingredients such as linseed and castor stand oil.

- Natural finishing oil can serve as a stand-alone primer, sealer, and protective layer for surfaces such as wood and cork.

- The thick, somewhat viscous oil preserves whatever surface it's applied to.

- Another advantage of natural oils is that they are VOC free.

finish has a satinlike patina.

Some of the most eco-friendly finishing materials can be combined to form other options. One example is a varnish oil that's a mix of highly polymerized linseed oil and natural resin. Building durability and sheen with each application, it has excellent abrasion- and scratch-resistance, making it a good choice for furniture and kitchen countertops. Other combinations include linseed oil and castor stand oil, which create a thick, penetrating liquid.

One of the most versatile finishes is wax, which can be applied to everything from cabinetry and paneling to furniture and floors. Easy to apply, a wax finish dries quickly and is simple to repair, if needed. Simply spread it in thin coats over a stain or sealer, then buff it out. Likewise, resin is versatile, too; it works on a wide variety of floor finishes. Given a resin finish, hardwood, softwood, even stone, brick, and cork take on a glossy sheen and a durable protective layer.

Wax

- Made up of a combination of beeswax and plant wax, this product adds a patina to wood like that found on antique furniture.

- Wax can be used on cork as well as wood surfaces, both on furniture and flooring.

- This type of finish is both durable and easy to apply.

- Wax can also be used to revive any other existing finish.

Resin

- Resin floor finishes range from clear to slightly amber in color.

- Applied in conjunction with a primer, resin provides a durable, glossy finish.

- It can be used on flooring of all kinds, including wood, stone, brick, and even cork.

- One or two coats of resin are usually sufficient for all but the most porous surfaces, like cork, which may require an extra application.

GROUT AND CAULK

When it comes to creating a green lifestyle, no detail is too small to overlook.

Just as important as the materials you choose is the grout and caulk that will hold everything together. Grout—a type of mortar used to fill joints, cracks, and cavities in tiles, masonry, and brick work—consists simply of water, cement, and/or sand. As basic as its formula is, however, it serves an important function. Sealed properly, grout retains its origi-nal color and keeps dirt from working its way between the tiles. Sealed improperly, however, the grout will easily stain and mold can even grow in damp areas. Of course, the less grout you use, the less chance there is of problems, too. By increasing the size of the tiles you use (for example, 12x12-inch instead of 6x6-inch), you'll reduce the number of grout

GREEN DECORATING & REMODELING

Grout

- Grout, in its most basic state, is similar in color to the sand and/or cement used to make it.

- Three types of grout are available: Portland cement-based, epoxy, and furan resin. Epoxy grout is a liquid form, while Portland cement-based and furan resin are available in sanded and unsanded types.

- Natural-colored grout is best, from a color point of view, used with tiles of similar neutral hues; the blended tones will make a floor, for instance, seem more expansive.

Colored Grout

- Cement-based and resin grouts are available not only in white but also in other hues such as black and terra-cotta.

- Colorants can also be added to white grout to make any imaginable shade.

- Color additives can be found in powdered form, similar to the grout itself.

- Colorants made specifically for grout are less likely to fade, unlike paint added to a mixed grout.

lines, too. Likewise, fewer grout lines result in the amount of VOCs that the grout and sealer will give off. To be on the same side, opt for those with low or no VOCs.

Water-based caulk, on the other hand, is a flexible sealant that can be used both indoors and out. It has versatility going for it, too. Caulk can tightly seal windows and doors, keeping heat in, as well as pipes and plumbing products, keeping water from running out. In short, this single product can add up to big savings.

············· YELLOW ● LIGHT ············

When using grout, it's particularly important to clean up correctly afterward. Do not pour the residue down a drain, as it could cause serious pipe damage. Instead, let the mixture sit long enough for the solids and liquids to separate. Once the elements have separated, you can pour the water off and throw the solid residue away.

Grout Sealer

- Sealers provide a clear, moisture-resistant coat atop porous tile grout.

- Some types actually react with and become part of the grout, further increasing water resistance and helping to prevent stains.

- Grout sealers are available that are formaldehyde free and all but odorless.

- These finishes can seal in any outgassing from the substance below.

Caulk

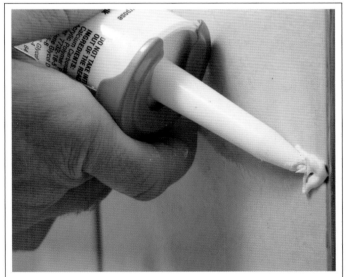

- Caulk can seal holes around windows, duct pipes, and masonry, not to mention tubs and showers.

- Caulk has elasticity. Because it stretches, it remains bonded as the materials next to it expand and contract with temperature changes.

- Caulk, a water-based product, can be painted, too.

- It is inexpensive and easy to use for any do-it-yourself.

PAINTS AND FINISHES

WALLPAPER

Today's wallpaper can give a room color, pattern, and a touch of green.

At first the words *green* and *wallpaper* may seem to be complete opposites. After all, how can a product that's printed with heavy dyes and applied with strong adhesives be part of an eco-friendly room? There is a way; it just takes looking a little harder for the right paper and paste. Don't be surprised when you turn up some cutting-edge options.

Some eco-friendly wallpapers are produced in traditional ways with natural materials (such as linseed oil) and hand-blocked patterns. Also look for those made of recycled content or printed on papers with an FSC (Forest Stewardship Council) seal. That's your assurance that the paper came from a well-managed forest. But the paper itself isn't the only consideration.

Grasscloth

- Grasscloth options, including jute, rush, and sea grass, now come in a wide array of colors, including coral and lilac, as well as prints.

- Bamboo is available in rolls, while bamboo tambour is generally sold by the panel.

- Raffia, woven out of banana and palm leaves, provides a textural option.

- Grasscloth's three-dimensional texture can disguise a wall's imperfections.

More Natural Materials

- Cork, shaved into thin veneers, can be laminated onto a paper backing to create an insulating wall covering.

- Hemp, a renewable resource, can be solidly laminated to a paper backing or applied in mosaic-like squares.

- Natural silk and linen wall coverings aren't inexpensive but add a luxurious look.

- Paper fibers can be woven into textured patterns, while natural rice paper and parchment have delicate textures all their own.

Also look for coverings with water-based inks and nontoxic finishes.

Natural fibers such as linen and silk make especially stunning wall coverings. And bamboo or grasscloth give a space casual elegance. Even cork can be translated into a striking wallpaper. Shaved into thin veneers and laminated to a backing, it can add warmth to a room—both physically and visually. When you stop to think about all of the green possibilities, the style options are all but endless.

Wallpaper

- Some of the most eco-friendly wallpapers are those produced in traditional ways with natural materials (such as linseed oil) and hand-blocked patterns.

- Look for papers that use water-based or low-VOC inks and nontoxic finishes.

- If possible, use papers from well-managed forests, too.

- To make your wall covering even greener, use nontoxic adhesives, too.

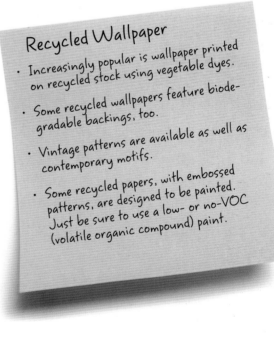

Recycled Wallpaper
- Increasingly popular is wallpaper printed on recycled stock using vegetable dyes.

- Some recycled wallpapers feature biodegradable backings, too.

- Vintage patterns are available as well as contemporary motifs.

- Some recycled papers, with embossed patterns, are designed to be painted. Just be sure to use a low- or no-VOC (volatile organic compound) paint.

49

WALL COVERINGS

PLASTER

The durability of plaster makes it eco-friendly, while the decorative possibilities make it eye-catching.

You may remember it from your grandmother's day and, with the growing popularity of plaster, your grandchildren will no doubt remember it from yours. Plaster's durability immediately makes it a green option; the fact that it can be patch-repaired—without replacing the wall covering entirely—even more so.

There are several options from which to choose. Plaster with a gypsum base has been around for ages. In fact, ancient Egyptians used it to plaster the great pyramid at Cheops. Today it's suitable for interior plastering, though it shouldn't be exposed to excessive moisture. Cement-based plaster, however, stands up to moisture well, and can be used

Gypsum Plaster

- Gypsum-based plasters are primarily reserved for indoor use, as excessive dampness may cause them to crumble.

- The most common gypsum plasters are browning, bonding, and metal lathing plaster.

- Today's plasters come premixed with perlite, vermiculite, and/or assorted other bonding agents.

- Additives to the mix can provide a greater degree of insulation and fire resistance.

Cement Plaster

- While cement-based plaster is primarily reserved for outdoor use, it's also appropriate indoors for areas that tend to get wet or stay damp.

- Cement-based plaster is also preferable where extra-thick walls are needed.

- Cement plasters can have a decorative purpose, too. Tuscany plaster has the look of honed stone, while Venetian Terra plaster has the look of stucco.

- Both Tuscany and Venetian plaster can be integrally colored and are available in a range of hues.

GREEN DECORATING & REMODELING

indoors or out. Plus it can serve a purely functional purpose or be more decorative. One of today's most popular wall finishes is Venetian plaster, which can be achieved with either cement- or lime-based products, and can be used to create highly polished smooth finishes or a more distressed look. This decorative technique can be multilayered, too, with accents, borders, and wax finishing coats.

Finally, clay plaster is as eco-friendly as any product you'll find. In commercial construction, the right clay plaster can even earn LEED (Leadership in Energy and Environmental Design) credits.

Lime Plaster

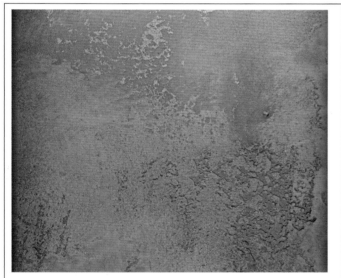

- Made up primarily of natural lime slake, lime-based plasters have a finish much like the sheen of marble.

- Marmorino plaster can have a range of textures including smooth, distressed, or stone-like, and the white base can be tinted in various hues.

- Veneciano plaster is an authentic lime-based plaster that consists of aged slaked lime and finely ground marble dust.

- Antico plaster contains finely ground dolomite, aged slaked lime, and fade-resistant pigments.

Clay Plaster

- In addition to natural clay, these plasters contain recycled and reclaimed aggregate and natural pigments.

- Finishes vary from very smooth to textured, and a wide variety of colors can be added to the base, too.

- Clay-based plasters are mold- and fade-resistant.

- Excess plaster can be reused, even after it's been mixed and has dried. After breaking the old plaster into pieces, it can simply be rehydrated.

WALL COVERINGS

TILE

There's no better way to express your own creativity than with tiled walls.

When selecting tile for wall applications, the possibilities are endless. Ceramic tile alone comes in every imaginable color and pattern. Today's ceramic tiles can take on the appearance of a wide variety of other materials. Instead of using exotic woods from endangered rain forests, use tiles that replicate the rich look. Likewise, there are tiles that mirror the images of river rock, stone, even leather. And don't forget about recycled options. More and more manufacturers are going the green route, creating tiles with some percentage of recycled content.

Porcelain is harder than ceramic tile, thus making it more durable—and greener in its own way. Like ceramic tile, how-

Ceramic Tile

- Ceramic tile retains heat and emits it slowly, which is especially good in climates that are warm during the day and cool at night.

- Although this material can be energy intensive to produce, it's offset by tile's durability.

- Ceramic tile is low maintenance; cleaning requires little more than a damp cloth.

- Tiles with a smooth surface are much easier to clean than those with textured patterns.

Porcelain Tile

- Porcelain is harder and denser than standard ceramic. It contains less clay and more of the mineral feldspar.

- Its density makes porcelain better for high-moisture areas such as bathrooms.

- Like conventional ceramic tile, porcelain is available in glazed and unglazed varieties; however, the shiny surface of glazed tiles are easier to keep clean.

- Porcelain is highly stain- and scratch-resistant.

ever, porcelain comes in a vast array of colors. And terra-cotta tiles are eco-friendly, too; they're often made up of nothing more than clay and water, although sometimes a little sand and/or soil is thrown into the mix. But before choosing any tile for your home, take time to think about more than its aesthetic appeal. It's just as important to look for types of tile that are appropriate to the application. Wall tiles are thinner—and therefore more lightweight—than tiles intended for the floor.

Terra-Cotta Tile

- Four basic materials make up terra-cotta—clay, sand, topsoil, and water.

- Depending on the clay that's used, terra-cotta tiles can range in color from a light reddish brown to nearly black.

- Terra-cotta is naturally hard as well as waterproof.

- In its natural state, terra-cotta has a matte finish, but it comes in colored glazes, too.

Recycled Tile

- Recycled ceramic tile is just as durable and stain resistant as its nonrecycled counterpart.

- The recycled content can be as much as 95 percent.

- Look for recycled ceramic tiles with glazes that have no lead or toxins.

- Reclaimed raw materials can also be used to create porcelain tiles; their recycled content is typically about 50 percent.

WALL COVERINGS

METAL AND GLASS

Tiles made of glass and metal can add immediate sparkle to any space.

Glass tiles are a bright idea for walls, not only because they shimmer but also because they're eco-friendly. The durability of glass tiles alone makes them green, but recycled glass tiles are even more so. They can be made of 100 percent postindustrial or postconsumer recycled content. (The glass you recycle could end up on your kitchen wall.) Plus, less energy is used to re-form glass into tiles than to create tiles from scratch. Likewise, metal tiles are rapidly gaining popularity, not only in contemporary spaces but also in more traditional installations. Like glass, metal tiles come in recycled forms, too. They're available in several colorful tints as well as more conventional metallic hues.

Glass Tile

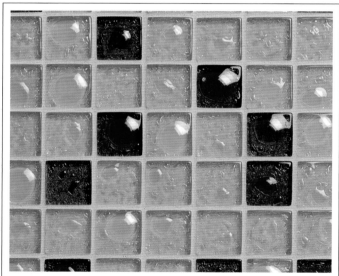

- Glass tile is not only durable but also easy to clean.

- Some glass tiles are fused, which requires less energy in the production process than conventional melting.

- Available in a vast array of colors, glass tile has a translucent and irridescent quality.

- Glass is impervious to moisture, making it a particularly good choice for kitchens and baths.

Recycled Glass Tile

- Recycled glass tiles can contain up to 100 percent recycled content.

- The amount of recycled content in a tile can vary greatly by its color. Manufacturers can provide specific percentages.

- Glass is recycled from various sources; some tiles, for instance, are the result of recycled window glass mixed with metallic oxides.

- Recycled green and brown bottles, typically the most difficult types to find new uses for, can be incorporated into recycled tiles.

In fact, practically any material that's appropriate as a wall covering can be cut into tile form. Concrete is a durable choice, offering earthy colors as well as unique shapes and textures. Wood tiles are another option; some are even made from furniture manufacturers' leftover scraps. Even bamboo and hand-stamped leather tiles are among the options today. Their beauty goes beyond being green. Because many tiles can be mixed and matched, you can create a one-of-a-kind wall covering.

Metal Tile

- Metal tiles can be found in a wide variety of materials, from brass and bronze to aluminum and stainless steel.

- Like almost all other tiles, metal types come in finishes ranging from matte to glossy.

- Beyond conventional squares, shapes include ovals, rounds, rectangles, and even octagons. Textured patterns are available, too.

- Metal tiles installed edge-to-edge reduce the grout used, as well as the likelihood of VOC emissions.

Recycled Metal Tile

- Using reclaimed materials, such as aluminum and brass, these metal tiles can contain up to 100 percent recycled content.

- Recycled metal tiles come in matte, polished, and sandblasted varieties.

- Nontoxic finishes prevent telltale fingerprints on metal tiles and can be maintained with a mild dish soap and water.

- Metal tiles, recycled or not, can also be used on countertops.

INVENTIVE WALL COVERINGS
It seems wall coverings are taking on a new twist at every turn.

The advances being made in wall coverings today are nothing short of sensational. Three-dimensional tiles, easy for the do-it-yourselfer to apply, are adding architectural interest at a phenomenal rate, while almost any material that can stand upright has taken on the role of decorative room divider. Something as simple as double-walled cardboard, for instance—the same type that's used in sturdy boxes—has taken an innovative turn. In at least one instance, recycled cardboard is being used to create modules that can be interlocked, creating portable walls that are as short or high, wide or narrow as you like. It's a solution especially well suited to open floor plans, like those in city lofts. Likewise, screens

Cardboard

- The "Nomad" wallboard system, like the one above, is made of recycled, double-walled cardboard board.

- The 21x4-inch modules can be assembled into freestanding screens or partitions.

- Available in six colors, sets of modules can be mixed and matched.

- No hardware, fasteners, or sealants are required for assembly, making it easy to put up and take down.

Wood and Rope

- Wood combines with simple cotton rope to create the "Piasa" room divider.

- The wood options (beech, maple, and cotton) are all FSC certified.

- Measuring 83 inches tall, the divider is available in widths anywhere from 6 to 30 feet long.

- The undulating form can be positioned in any number of ways.

made of nothing more than wood and rope can serve as handsome room dividers. And because the rope that holds the wood panels together has so much flexibility, this type of screen can take almost any form.

Walls need not be freestanding to be three-dimensional, either. You'll find three-dimensional wall tiles made of recycled paper that are easy to apply yourself. The tiles can be painted, but be sure to use a paint with low or no VOCs, not only for a healthier room but also so you can safely recycle the tiles when you're through. If you're looking for a more permanent wall treatment, however, there's nothing much more so than concrete. In lieu of the real thing, consider Eco-Cem, a concrete-like substance that can take the form of sturdy wall panels. What's interesting about this product, in addition to the fact that it can be colored, is that its makeup includes cellulose, which allows it to develop a soft patina over time. In the realm of wall coverings, it seems creativity is only at its peak.

Wallpaper Tiles

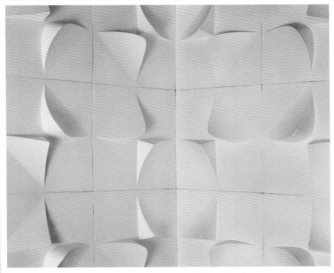

- Made entirely of recycled paper, the "V2" wallpaper tiles are also recyclable.

- The three-dimensional 12-inch-square tiles can be configured in any number of ways.

- Although they come in white, the tiles can be painted, too.

- Water-based paint can be brushed, rolled, or sprayed onto the tiles.

A Concrete Alternative

- Eco-Cem, a concrete-like substance, can be used to create sturdy wall panels.

- Given its high percentage of cellulose fibers, the material develops a patina over time.

- Eco-Cem can be sealed or left untreated.

- Because the material isn't stain resistant, spills need to be cleaned up immediately.

SHADES

The right window shades can make a big impact on your energy bill as well as your decor.

Shades are one of the most efficient options in terms of window treatments. They have great insulating value because they are positioned so closely to the glass. Plus, their decorative options are more far-reaching than ever before.

Roller shades, for instance, have come a long way since the days when the all-white vinyl variety dressed your grand-mother's windows. Today's versions come in any number of natural fabrics, many with trim just as natural as the shade itself. Roman shades have even more decorative options; you can find them in a wide variety of ready-made options but can have custom shades made in your choice of fabrics, too.

Roller Shades

- Roller shades have come a long way since the days of white-only vinyl options. Today's offerings, many of which are in natural fabrics, are available in a wide assortment of patterns and colors.

- The rollers are typically made of wood or steel.

- Because roller shades are basically a single flat panel, they're an economical choice, too.

- To further increase a shade's insulative value, or double a window's decorative impact, it can be teamed up with complementary curtains.

Roman Shades

- Like roller shades, Romans consist of a flat piece of fabric. Instead of rolling up, however, they pull up to the top of the window in soft folds.

- The close proximity of a Roman shade to the window makes it an energy-saving option.

- The flat construction of a Roman shade lends itself to almost any fabric.

- Because Roman shades have rings attached to the backs (for pull-up cords to go through), they generally must be professionally cleaned.

Solar shades provide the best of two worlds: blocking out the sun's glare while still letting light filter in. Blackout shades not only darken a room but provide sound insulation, too. And for those with sensitivities to human-made fibers, keep in mind that solar and blackout shades typically contain PVC and/or vinyl of some kind. For those not sensitive to the materials, though, these specialty shades are good choices given the amount of energy they save. In short, today's window shades provide fashion and function, all "rolled up" into one.

MAKE IT EASY

Not all roller shades pull down from the top of the window. If you need privacy but still want a partial view, opt for shades that pull from the bottom up.

Solar Shades

- Woven solar shades keep out the sun's heat and glare while still allowing light to gently filter into a room.

- Light-colored shades, such as white and cream, are best for holding off heat. Dark colors typically cut the glare better and allow the best outdoor view.

- Solar shades keep upholstery fabrics from fading.

- Most woven solar shades can easily be cleaned with soap and water.

Blackout Shades

- Blackout shades are a good choice for rooms that need to be completely dark, such as a media room or the bedroom.

- While blocking out light, these window treatments provide some sound insulation, too.

- Blackout shades are available in a wide range of fabrics.

- Side panels are sometimes available, reducing the possibility of light leaking in.

NATURAL FIBERS

Traditional natural-fiber window shades put an inventive twist on style.

The beauty of woven-fiber shades goes beyond the fact that they're all natural. Rattan, bamboo, sea grass, hemp, and wood-fiber varieties can be constructed in myriad patterns and are relatively easy to install yourself. The increasing number of natural fibers being woven into window treatments not only provides a greater variety of textures today, but the color palette has expanded accordingly, too. No longer are woven shades limited to a medium brown tone. Now, you're just as likely to find everything from soft creams to pale grays to sage greens. And, of course, you can find brown in every shade imaginable, from brown sugar to chocolate.

Rattan is one of the most popular natural fibers used for

Rattan

- Rattan window treatments are widely available in shade form, which pull up and fold much like Romans.

- Other rattan options include blinds and sliding screens.

- Natural fibers like rattan allow filtered sunlight to shine through. However, privacy lining can be added, if necessary.

- Rattan blinds and shades can cost as much as four times what comparable vinyl blinds do.

Bamboo

- Bamboo's durability makes it a good choice. It can outlast many of its vinyl and aluminum counterparts.

- The slats of a bamboo blind can vary greatly, from matchstick-thin to wider, strawlike versions.

- How tightly the slats are woven together dictates how much, or how little, light can enter the room.

- The control mechanism at the top of a bamboo shade is sometimes concealed by a matching valance, attached to the shade itself.

window shades. In addition to conventional Roman-style shades, rattan—in the form of moveable panels—can dress sliding patio doors, too. Not surprisingly, either, bamboo is showing up in an increasing number of window shades; its durability and sustainability is hard to beat.

When it comes to window treatments, those made of hemp may not be the first ones to come to mind. That's rapidly changing, though, as this inexpensive material becomes more readily available. In fact, as technology continues to improve, don't be surprised to see any natural fiber show up in window shade form. Sea grass and jute shades are already prevalent, as are those made of wood fiber and flax. In addition to being eco-friendly, natural-fiber shades feature warm neutral hues that are compatible with virtually any decor, whether used alone or teamed up with soft curtains or draperies.

Hemp

- Shades made of eco-friendly hemp are a natural; the material easily falls into Roman-style folds.

- In most hemp shades, the fabric is left in its natural off-white color.

- Top-down and bottom-up versions are both readily available.

- Insulating and blackout linings can be added to hemp shades.

More Wonderful Wovens

- Sea grass is increasingly popular as a floor covering, but it can be crafted into casual window shades, too.

- Shades featuring wood reeds can be stained or left in their natural state.

- Jute fibers can be used on their own or teamed up with other natural materials, such as sisal and sea grass.

- Flax, in its more natural grasslike state, can take the form of bleached, natural-colored, or deep brown shades.

BLINDS AND SHUTTERS

More than purely practical, blinds and shutters enhance a room's architectural aspect.

GREEN DECORATING & REMODELING

If your priority is to control light and privacy, blinds and shutters can't be beat. Their adjustable vanes can be leveled, allowing sunlight to virtually flood a space. Likewise, these treatments can be completely closed, shielding the room and its occupants not only from Mother Nature's forces but also from passersby. The fact that blinds and shutters are striking, too, is practically a bonus.

Wood blinds are perennial favorites in traditional rooms, but there's no need to limit them to areas decorated in that one specific style. Because they come in such a vast array of colors, from subtle neutrals to vibrant brights, wood blinds can enhance nearly any room. Similarly, Venetian blinds

Wood Blinds

- Window blinds are available in a variety of woods, including ash, oak, and cherry. Their natural beauty can lend warmth to a room.

- Less-costly species, such as basswood, are available, too, and can be finished in a wide variety of wood stains.

- Custom blinds can be made to fit any window, including those that are arched or round.

- Although wood blinds are more expensive, they pay for themselves in terms of longevity and the amount of energy they can save.

Venetian Blinds

- Like wood blinds, the Venetian variety features slats that can be open, closed, or somewhere in between.

- Venetian blinds have good energy efficiency and sound absorption, though not as much as their wood counterparts.

- Venetian blinds, typically made of aluminum, come in a wide variety of colors. They can be customized with tapes in a multitude of colors. Most are the same kind of cotton twill found in vintage treatments.

adapt well to any space. The vanes of these blinds range from as narrow as 1 inch up to 3 inches wide, the latter having a look similar to vintage blinds. Both wood and Venetian blinds have energy-saving aspects, too; because the vanes close tightly, a room's heat—or air-conditioning—is less likely to go right out the window.

Shutters, for that matter, have the same advantage. Because shutters are attached directly to a window frame, though, they also add architectural interest to a room. Standard shutters feature louvers that are approximately 1¼ inches wide, while plantation shutters have wider louvers, ranging from 2½ to 4½ inches wide. Their larger scale makes them a particularly good choice for contemporary homes with over-scaled windows. Plus, the bigger the louvers, the more light that's allowed indoors when they're completely open. If you like the look of shutters, but not the expense, consider shutters made of extruded foam. The material may not be natural, but it is durable and nontoxic, which make a difference in the green movement, too.

Wood Shutters

- Wood shutters, made of species such as basswood and certain hardwoods, add architectural interest to a room.

- The wood vanes can be painted or stained to enhance the natural grain.

- Like wood blinds, shutters can be customized to any window shape and size.

- Although more expensive than wood blinds, classic wood shutters are durable as well as energy efficient.

Other Shutters

- As an alternative to wood shutters, you'll also find those made of extruded foam.

- Although crafted of a human-made material, these shutters still have the appearance of wood.

- This specialty material is nontoxic.

- Because these shutters stand up well to adverse weather, they can be used indoors and out.

MORE WINDOW DRESSINGS

Whether your design preference is classic or cutting-edge, there's a green window treatment to suit your style.

Window treatments are really only limited by two things: your specific needs and your imagination. From stained glass and tried-and-true window quilts that have been used for generations to more up-to-the-minute window film and sustainable solar shades, there's a good solution to any green lifestyle. It's merely a matter of picking your priorities.

The popularity of stained glass continues to grow, not only because it's decorative but also due to the fact that it's a natural sun blocker; the darker the color of the glass, the more harmful UV rays it reflects. And window quilts are one of the best insulators you'll find. When pulled all the way down, these window treatments have the ability to seal on

Window Quilts

- Window quilts are one of the most energy-efficient window treatments; because they seal on all four sides, window quilts can save up to 80 percent of a window's heat loss.

- These roll-up shades are often concealed under a matching valance.

- Fabrics used in window quilts are typically a cotton-polyester combination.

- This multiple-layered fabric treatment is available in a variety of colors and patterns; room-darkening fabrics are optional, too.

Stained Glass

- The cost of creating a stained-glass window is comparable to other high-quality window treatments.

- The amount of sunlight shielded by a stained-glass window is color dependent; the darker the hues, the more light that's kept out.

- Stained-glass windows are easy to maintain; they require nothing different than standard glass.

- These window treatments can be made of recycled glass and also be recycled in the future.

all four sides, saving up to an impressive 80 percent of a window's potential heat loss. For window treatments that block a good deal of the sun, but not the view, window film and solar shades are also energy-efficient solutions.

But when deciding which window treatment is right for you, don't forget about the vast recycling possibilities, either. Vintage tablecloths, for instance, like those used in the 1950s, can be transformed into colorful curtains. Even your grandmother's handkerchiefs can be used to create a delicate valance.

ZOOM

Low-E glass has what's referred to as "low emissivity," due to a film or metallic coating on the glass that reflects the sun's rays and keeps out radiant heat. This type of coating can reflect between 40 and 70 percent of transmitted heat while still allowing natural light to come through the window.

Window Film

- Applied directly to the glass, window film is one of the most energy-efficient options.

- In addition to its insulative value, window film provides UV protection that's superior to most Low-E glass.

- It also reduces glare and keeps fabrics from fading.

- An added benefit is that the film helps strengthen a window's glass panes.

Sustainable Solar Shades

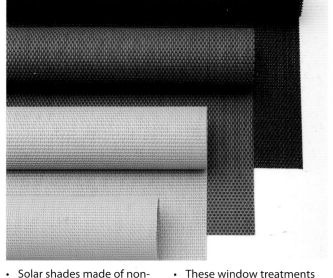

- Solar shades made of non-PVC (polyvinyl chloride) cloth are environmentally friendly.

- In addition to shielding the sun's rays, these shades are durable and washable.

- These window treatments are flame-retardant.

- Non-PVC solar shades can be reclaimed and recycled.

COTTON

As a natural choice for rugs, cotton offers a cushy comfort underfoot.

There's just something about walking barefoot across a rug or carpet, your toes digging into the nap with each comfy step. What can make it even more comforting are soft floor coverings that are green. These eco-friendly alternatives are more extensive than you may think.

When it comes to cotton, look for styles that are 100 percent fiber. Although conventional cotton may have been sprayed with pesticides during the growing process, the fact that it's a natural fiber still takes you to the first step in going green. Organic cotton rugs are a better choice, although at this point they're primarily limited to bathroom and small rag rugs. Still, a third option is to use soft floor

Cotton

- Some of the simplest all-cotton rugs include rag and braided versions. More luxurious styles encompass hand-hooked designs and sculpted patterns.

- Cotton rugs come in various textures, too, from stretchy strips of jersey to plush chenille.

- Because they're water-absorbent, cotton rugs are good choices for kitchens and baths.

- Many flat-woven cotton rugs are reversible, which lets you get twice the wear from them.

Organic Cotton

- Rugs made of extra-soft organic cotton are a good choice for a nursery or child's room as well as the kitchen or bathroom.

- The color palette is more limited than for rugs made of conventional cotton.

- Taking the green concept one step further, some rugs are made with recycled scraps of organic cotton.

- Organic cotton rugs are durable and washable.

coverings made of recycled cotton.

The choices you'll find in color, pattern, and texture are literally enough to make your head spin. But unless your rug has a nonslip backing, the floor covering itself is just half the story. Whether your rug is going atop a hardwood floor or a plush carpet, a rug pad is required beneath it. A pad keeps the rug from sliding across a hard surface and from "creeping" across a carpeted one. The pad may not be made of natural materials (and many aren't), but the tradeoff is in the interest of your safety.

Recycled Cotton

- Rugs made of recycled cotton can be even more comfy than their conventional counterparts, because cotton gets softer over time.

- Recycled cotton rugs can be made of scraps from various resources, such as T-shirts and blue jeans.

- Even fabric selvedges, collected from weaving mills can be transformed into new rugs.

- Recycled cotton rugs are just as durable as those that are brand-new.

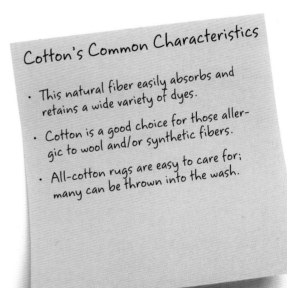

Cotton's Common Characteristics

- This natural fiber easily absorbs and retains a wide variety of dyes.

- Cotton is a good choice for those allergic to wool and/or synthetic fibers.

- All-cotton rugs are easy to care for; many can be thrown into the wash.

WOOL
Wool floor coverings provide a warmth that's beyond compare.

Wool and *luxurious* are all but synonymous, especially when it comes to carpet and rugs. Like cotton, wool can be flat-woven, its fluffy fibers providing warmth underfoot. But wool is, perhaps, at its best in hand-knotted and thickly tufted floor coverings, whether it's a needlepoint rug, a shag rug, or a wall-to-wall plush.

Because wool is a great insulator, it's a logical choice for floor coverings. On a hard surface floor, particularly, it provides warmth underfoot. Look for rugs that utilize vegetable dyes or opt for floor coverings made of all-natural wool, their colors provided by nothing more than the original shade of the sheep's wool. When shopping for wool rugs, however,

Wool

- Wool rugs can take the form of everything from traditional Oriental rugs to more contemporary designs.

- Wool is resistant to dirt, making it easy to clean. The compact nature of its fibers makes it harder for dirt to work its way down into the rug.

- The natural beauty of wool actually increases over time, developing a soft patina.

- As a rule, rugs made of wool require professional cleaning.

Natural Wool

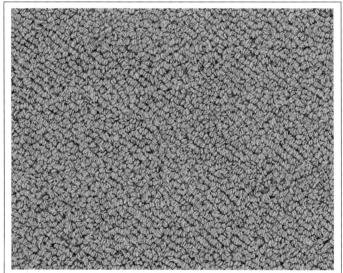

- All-natural carpet takes on the color of the raw wool, which can range from creamy white to dark brown.

- No moth-proofing or stain protectors are applied, or needed, in wool rugs.

- In a true all-natural product, backings are made of hemp, cotton, jute, and/or natural rubber.

- Even the adhesives are all natural, making the product biodegradable.

watch out for toxic chemicals that may have been applied for mothproofing purposes. Recycled wool rugs, on the other hand, rarely have any kind of toxic additives. Because the wool used for recycled floor coverings has often seen another use first, it can be even softer than if it were new. Some even have a comforting vintage appearance, looking like giant versions of the woven pot holders.

Wool may be a bit more expensive than other soft floor coverings, but it will withstand the test of time, making this fiber a sound investment.

·········· GREEN ● LIGHT ··············

The Carpet and Rug Institute (CRI) has established a Green Label program that identifies products with low-VOC (volatile organic compound) emissions. It also launched Green Label Plus, an enhanced program for carpet and adhesives that sets the bar even higher to ensure that customers are purchasing the lowest-emitting products on the market. Look for the label!

Recycled Wool

- Like their cotton counterparts, recycled wool rugs can come from various sources.

- Some recycled rugs took the form of another product in a previous "life," while others are made of never-before-used scraps.

- Reclaimed sweaters make some of the softest recycled rugs.

- Some recycled wool rugs can be washed versus having them professionally cleaned.

Wool's Common Characteristics

- Wool is known for its luxurious look and its durability.

- Like other natural fibers, wool accepts color well.

- Rugs made of wool are typically more expensive than those made of synthetic or other natural materials.

- Wool is resilient and is naturally resistant to fire, water, and stains.

73

SISAL AND SEA GRASS

Rugs made of natural fibers like sisal and sea grass add striking texture to a room.

No longer reserved only for casual rooms, sisal is now at home throughout the house. (In fact, you can find wool that replicates sisal's natural pattern and color.) And sea grass isn't far behind. These kinds of natural fibers can be dressed up or down. Either way, they're relatively inexpensive, so they won't make much of a dent in your budget.

Although sisal flooring has a distinct texture, it doesn't trap dust as you might expect. Plus, sisal is extremely durable, so it's a good fit for almost any space. In fact, bathrooms and kids' rooms are about the only areas that are off-limits. Sisal is susceptible to mildew, so it needs to be put in a dry location. Likewise, the same texture that is so visually appealing

Natural Sisal

- Sisal, made from the leaves of the agave plant, is one of the most popular plant fibers used for rugs.

- These rugs are antistatic, sound absorbing, and flame-retardant.

- Sisal is a good choice for high-traffic areas.

- Sisal flooring should not be installed on stairways, because over time the material can become slippery.

- Because sisal has a course texture, it's not the best choice if there are small children, especially those just learning to crawl.

Sisal + Pattern and Color

- Sisal can be woven to create a variety of textured patterns, such as jacquard and herringbone.

- Woven patterns can be subtle, in natural sisal shades, or made more prominent by dying some of the fibers.

- Pattern can also be applied to the face of the floor covering. Stripes and checkerboards are common.

- Solid-color or patterned-fabric borders can also be added to sisal rugs.

can be hard on the hands and knees of children who like to play on the floor.

Sea grass rugs, like those made of sisal, should be reserved for indoor use; although the fibers are durable, they will break down quickly if they're exposed to the elements. Indoors, however, it's a versatile floor covering. Because sea grass has a neutral soft green color, it complements just about any scheme. In fact, thanks to its natural beauty, sea grass is rarely dyed. Still, you will find sea grass—as well as sisal—in a variety of colors and patterns, too. Whether you opt for sisal and sea grass in their natural states or more colorful forms, rest assured that you'll be getting a floor covering that's fashionable, functional, and, just as important, comfortable underfoot.

Look for sisal and sea grass rugs backed with natural latex, or rubber.

Sea Grass

- Sea grass, made from a tall plant found in wetlands, is characterized by grass-like stems.

- Rugs made of sea grass have a naturally smooth texture.

- This type of floor covering can be identified by a hay-like smell and hue, both of which typically fade over time.

Sea Grass + Pattern and Color

- The natural variations of color in sea grass can be woven into assorted patterns.

- Sea grass, itself, cannot be dyed; the fiber is impermeable.

- Strands of other colored fibers can be woven into the floor covering.

- Like sisal, rugs made of sea grass can be bound with a decorative edging.

COIR AND JUTE
The coarse fibers of coir and jute can add up to refined style.

In casual settings, coir and jute rugs look good on their own or layered atop another floor covering, whether it's hardwood or something softer such as berber carpet. These natural-fiber options add textural interest that complements furnishings of any style.

Coir is also known as coco fiber, because it comes from the fibrous husk of the coconut. One of the most durable natural fibers, coir can stand up to daily wear and tear, which makes it a good rug material. Plus, this fiber is naturally insulating and sound absorbing, as well as antistatic and fire resistant. On the other hand, you may be more familiar with jute in its more common incarnation—burlap. Made with rough wo-

GREEN DECORATING & REMODELING

Natural Coir

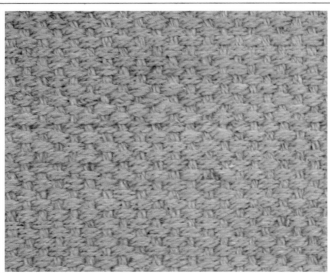

- Coir is made from the discarded husks of coconuts.

- Rugs made of coir typically have a latex backing, but its coarse texture often requires a protective rug pad, too.

- The inherent texture of coir, plus its slight color variations, adds up to layers of visual interest.

- Be mindful of rug placement; coir rugs that are exposed to direct sunlight will change in color over time.

Coir + Color and Pattern

- Whether in its natural brown or dyed another hue, coir has color variations throughout the fiber.

- Coir fibers can be dyed to create rugs in stripes, herringbone, even kilim-like patterns.

- Cotton twill tape, in various colors, is often used to edge coir rugs for added visual appeal.

- Coir can be coupled with other natural fibers, like sisal, to create interesting textures and add durability.

ven jute, burlap has been appreciated for years for its nearly indestructible character, which translates to floor coverings, too. This natural fiber, derived from a woody herb found in India, is completely biodegradable and versatile. It can be spun into very fine yarns, creating a rug with a fine texture, or into heavy cords that create a more casual look.

Like sisal and sea grass, coir and jute rugs are readily found in their natural colors, or with eye-catching color and pattern, too.

> ### GREEN ● LIGHT
>
> The naturally coarse texture of coir makes it a good choice for **door mats**, too; by wiping your feet on the fibers, dirt brushes off and falls down into the rug. Better yet, all it takes is a quick shake to clean it out.

Natural Jute

- Because the fibers come from the plant stalk instead of the leaves, jute is softer than some other natural fibers.

- Jute, in its natural state, is brown.

- Rugs made of jute are not as durable as some other natural options, but do hold up well under low to medium traffic.

- Be careful of spills; jute can be susceptible to stains.

Jute + Color and Pattern

- Like cotton and wool, jute rugs can be found in hand-knotted or handwoven versions.

- Jute can be dyed to take on other earthy colors and even jewel tones.

- Patterns, such as stripes, can be interwoven for added variety.

- Cotton binding tapes, available in a wide variety of colors, are often used to edge natural fiber rugs such as jute.

MORE SOFT SOLUTIONS

When it comes to soft floor coverings, the green possibilities are greater than ever.

The types of materials being transformed into floor coverings are all but mind-boggling. Paper, hemp, silk, and all manner of recycled items are taking shape as some of today's most innovative offerings. Some replicate the look of less-than-eco-friendly options, providing the opportunity to get the look you want in a green way.

While paper probably isn't a material you'd think of as a floor covering, it makes sense from an eco-friendly point of view. As the working world goes more electronic and less paper dependent, the durable fiber is increasingly available for other uses. Don't be surprised, either, by the wide variety of colors and textures you'll find. Hemp, on the other hand,

Paper

- Twisted paper fiber is now being used to create novel floor coverings.

- Paper flooring is soft and smooth underfoot, even more so when it's combined with other natural fibers such as wool.

- A wax emulsion is often added to paper floorings to make them water-resistant.

- Look for rugs made of pulp taken from trees of responsibly managed forests.

Hemp

- Hemp rugs are typically found in their undyed, natural state.

- This natural fiber is anti-static and stain resistant.

- Hemp is durable, withstanding even high-traffic areas.

- Because this fiber can be susceptible to mold and mildew, don't use hemp rugs in damp settings.

is more often found in its natural, all-white color. There's something to be said for neutrals, though: They go with anything.

Silk, at the high end of the luxury spectrum, has been used for centuries to weave exotic Oriental rugs. Today, however, you'll also find other incarnations of this luxurious fiber—even scraps woven into jewel-toned rugs. It's not all that shocking, once you stop to think about it. One of the best things to come out of the green movement is that we're looking at materials in new ways.

Silk

- Silk rugs are most commonly Oriental-style floor coverings.

- The rug's pile as well as the base are pure silk; no wool or cotton is used.

- These hand-knotted rugs are characterized by intricate patterns.

- Silk fibers can take more contemporary forms, too. Recycled silk remnants can be woven into rag rugs.

Recycled Fibers

- Wool and cotton are two common materials used to make recycled rugs.

- Rugs are also being woven using leftover remnants from clothing mills (think blue jeans) and even bedding factories.

- Great strides have been made in indoor/outdoor rugs. Made of recycled plastic bottles and packing materials, they can be washed off with a hose.

- Recycled indoor/outdoor rugs don't absorb stains, either, and won't trap water or mildew.

CARPET PADS

Even in the eco-friendly arena, not all carpet pads are created equal.

Now that you've found the perfect carpet, one that suits your design sensibilities as well as your lifestyle, don't let your hard work be for naught by choosing the wrong pad to put beneath. Wool, cotton, jute, natural rubber, and recycled carpet pads all have their own advantages. Choose the one that works best with your floor treatment.

The right carpet or rug pad will do more than provide comfort underfoot. Because it acts as a shock absorber, a carpet pad will extend the life of your floor covering, too. Plus, it helps buffer sound and adds another layer of insulation. While rug pads are pretty universal, carpet pads should be selected with care. The type and thickness required de-

Wool

- Premium wool pads are typically made with virgin fibers, though some can include up to 80 percent preconsumer waste.

- Look for wool padding that is mechanically needled, not glued, to a jute backing.

- Wool carpet pads are resilient and durable, standing up well in high-traffic rooms.

- Some wool pads, after serving their initial use, can be spread in the garden to serve as a weed barrier while gradually decomposing.

Rubber

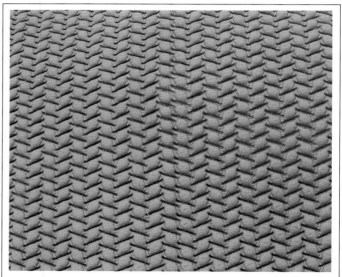

- Carpet pads made of natural rubber provide a comfortable, nonskid basis for rugs and carpet.

- Pads made of 100 percent rubber will not stain floors.

- The material can be easily cut, making it a snap to fit any size floor covering.

- Precut sizes are also available.

pends, a great deal, on where the floor covering will be used. Spaces that get only light or moderate traffic, like bedrooms, can handle thicker, softer padding, while high-traffic rooms and hallways require pads that are thinner and firmer. Make it a point to check the manufacturer's requirements for the recommended type of carpet pad. The wrong choice can cause a carpet to wear down quickly, buckling and even separating at the seams.

You'll find recycled pads made of synthetic fibers reclaimed from carpet mills an especially good choice for rugs made of natural fibers. Because these pads are typically bonded by heat, they're free of toxic adhesives, too. Like any other type of pad, however, they are available in a variety of thicknesses.

Jute

- Jute carpet pads are both natural and biodegradable.

- This type of pad has good thermal and acoustic insulation.

- Because jute pads have low toxicity, they're a good choice for those who are sensitive to chemicals.

- The thickness of a jute carpet pad can help level an uneven floor.

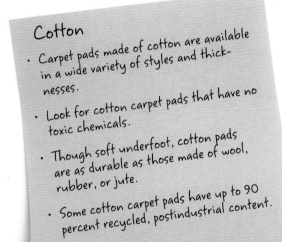

Cotton
- Carpet pads made of cotton are available in a wide variety of styles and thicknesses.

- Look for cotton carpet pads that have no toxic chemicals.

- Though soft underfoot, cotton pads are as durable as those made of wool, rubber, or jute.

- Some cotton carpet pads have up to 90 percent recycled, postindustrial content.

WOOD

Natural wood can provide a beautiful basis for almost any room.

Gleaming wood floors offer a world of decorative opportunities. The number of species you can choose from is impressive alone, but there are various types of wood floors to consider, too. Are you looking for a solid-wood floor? Engineered wood flooring? Or would you prefer reclaimed wood? Each type has its advantages, and all are stunning on their own or coupled with a handsome area rug.

Solid-wood floors have classic good looks. And because they don't collect dust and other allergens, they have a health benefit, too. Look for lumber taken from responsibly managed forests, like those with FSC (Forest Stewardship Council) certification. If your floor needs to be extrasturdy, you

Solid Wood

- Solid-wood flooring is one piece of wood from top to bottom regardless of the width or length.

- The most common wood species used for solid strip floors are red oak, white oak, maple, cherry, white ash, hickory, and pecan.

- Look for species from well-managed forests.

- Flooring made of solid wood comes prefinished or unfinished.

- Solid-wood floors are sensitive to moisture and are not recommended for below-ground installations.

Engineered Wood

- Engineered wood floors are generally manufactured in three- or five-ply sheets laminated together to form one plank.

- Engineered wood floors replicate the look of many of their solid counterparts; some of the finishes include cherry, maple, and oak.

- Because the grains run in different directions, engineered wood is more dimensionally stable than solid wood.

- This type of flooring is good for areas where solid wood may not be suitable, such as basements, kitchens, and powder and utility rooms.

may want to consider engineered wood. Made of planks laminated together, engineered wood looks just like the solid variety, but it's more dimensionally stable. That makes it an especially good choice for kitchens, bathrooms, or anywhere that gets wet.

Without a doubt, though, reclaimed wood is the most eco-friendly option. The fact that wood can see a lifetime of use in one building, then be salvaged and adapted to another, proves unquestionably that wood lives up to the green standard of durability, too.

The finish you choose for your floor is just as important as the wood itself. Look for water-based urethane finishes; they're nonyellowing, have a milder odor than solvent-based varnishes, and typically dry in two to three hours.

Reclaimed Wood

- Reclaimed wood flooring is remilled from tight-grained, old-growth lumber taken from deconstructed buildings.

- Some reclaimed wood is also retrieved from waterways.

- Nail holes and other marks are considered part of the rustic appeal.

- Forest salvage is an alternative to conventionally reclaimed wood. It is cut from trees that are dead but still standing or that have been knocked down by the wind.

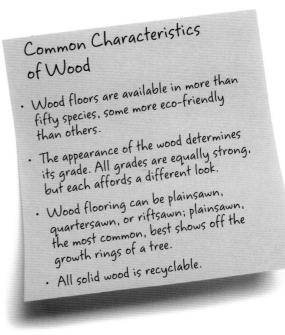

Common Characteristics of Wood

- Wood floors are available in more than fifty species, some more eco-friendly than others.

- The appearance of the wood determines its grade. All grades are equally strong, but each affords a different look.

- Wood flooring can be plainsawn, quartersawn, or riftsawn; plainsawn, the most common, best shows off the growth rings of a tree.

- All solid wood is recyclable.

BAMBOO

Bamboo, a grass, is one of the most durable floorings you'll find.

The ways in which bamboo can be used increase every day. But one of the best ways is right at your feet. Bamboo flooring is available in a natural state, with both engineered and strand-woven options out there, too. And if bamboo's good looks alone aren't enough to grab you, consider this: Bamboo is touted as the world's fastest-growing plant, making it incredibly sustainable, and it has a tensile strength comparable to steel.

Natural bamboo flooring can have the appearance of flattened bamboo stalks, referred to as horizontal boards, or something that looks more like wood, known as vertical flooring. Horizontal bamboo is well suited to casual settings,

GREEN DECORATING & REMODELING

Natural

- Bamboo flooring is available in two basic constructions—horizontal and vertical.

- Horizontal boards are manufactured by laminating three layers of bamboo side by side, creating a look similar to flattened bamboo stalks.

- Vertical boards are created by turning the bamboo strips ninety degrees and positioning them next to each other.

- Horizontal construction is typically harder and more stable than the vertical option.

Engineered

- Engineered bamboo floors feature a thin layer of bamboo laminated over a nonbamboo material.

- Tongue-and-groove flooring is made from bamboo-oriented strand board (OSB), crafted from post-industrial-waste bamboo.

- Engineered bamboo floors can be installed on top of concrete or wood subfloors.

- Look for bamboo floors with adhesives that have no formaldehyde.

while vertical pieces, in more formal rooms, may well be mistaken for wood. Engineered and strand-woven bamboo flooring are both created via a laminating process. Because adhesives are a necessary part of the procedure, look for flooring made with nontoxic types.

Another option is hand-scraped bamboo floors, which have an antique-looking quality much like reclaimed wood. This type of flooring, though, comes at a price, primarily because it takes about ten times longer to produce a hand-scraped plank than it does a plank of solid or engineered bamboo.

Strand Woven

- Strand-woven bamboo is made by heating long strips of bamboo, weaving them together, and then laminating them.

- This process makes it harder and denser than traditional bamboo flooring.

- Strand-woven floors have a distinct grain that's similar to that of hardwood.

- The durability of strand-woven bamboo makes it a good choice in a home with kids or pets.

Common Characteristics of Bamboo

- An eco-friendly alternative to conventional hardwood, bamboo grass is fast growing and ready to harvest after just three to five years.

- Bamboo floors are maintained in the same way as wood floors and can be refinished.

- Bamboo comes in various grades, differentiating hardness and quality.

- Bamboo flooring ranges in color from very light to dark brown shades.

HARD FLOOR COVERINGS

LINOLEUM AND RUBBER

All-natural linoleum and rubber, in their various forms, are both good-looking and green.

A relative newcomer and a tried-and-true returnee, rubber and linoleum both offer flooring that's not only easy on the eyes but easy to live with, too. Their resiliency gives them an extra measure of comfort, something to consider in the kitchen, for instance, where you tend to stand for long stretches at time. Add to that their easy-care aspect, and you've got flooring options worth a hard look.

True linoleum couldn't be greener, made of nothing more than natural—and renewable—resources. Its most recent wave of popularity has resulted in flooring in every imaginable color. But beware of linoleum wannabes. The word *linoleum* is often used incorrectly to describe any type of sheet

Natural Linoleum

Colored Linoleum

- True linoleum is all natural, made of materials such as linseed oil, pine resin, wood flour, cork flour, limestone, and jute.

- Linoleum is available in sheet goods as well as plank and tile form.

- To clean, all it needs is a dry mop or broom and, occasionally, a wet mopping.

- Linoleum is biodegradable, formaldehyde free, and nontoxic, although even some of the natural oils can outgas, which might be a concern for those with chemical sensitivities.

- Linoleum is offered in many more colors today than when it was first introduced in 1863, ranging from sunflower yellow to sapphire blue.

- Linoleum in any color is both antistatic and antibacterial.

- Due to its durability, linoleum has been dubbed by some as the "forty-year floor," because it gets tougher with time as the linseed oil cures.

- Some linoleum flooring is FSC certified. Check with your local retailer.

goods, when, in fact, the flooring may be made from other materials such as vinyl and PVC (polyvinyl chloride).

Rubber flooring for residential use is a relative newcomer, having made the transition from industrial buildings. If this type of floor can stand up to commercial use, you know that it can take anything your home can dish out. While you might expect it to come in standard black, today's color choices—in new rubber flooring as well as recycled—are anything but ordinary. Put a bright yellow rubber floor in the kitchen and a blue or pink one in your child's playroom. The sky's the limit!

ZOOM

Due to its natural components, linoleum's surface may yellow when it's first taken out of the packaging. This temporary situation will be remedied once the new floor is exposed to sunlight. The amount of time it will take your floor to "bloom"—or take on its true color—depends on how much light it gets.

Rubber

- Rubber flooring is a good choice for kitchens and baths as well as laundry rooms, play rooms, and home offices.

- This type of floor is available in sheet form as well as tiles.

- Rubber flooring comes in a wide variety of colors and a number of embossed patterns, too.

- The only maintenance rubber floors require is an occasional washing.

Recycled Rubber

- Recycled rubber floors are typically a blend of recycled tires, postindustrial-waste rubber, and virgin rubber.

- Like all-natural rubber, the recycled variety is durable and easy to maintain.

- This type of flooring can be found in sheet goods as well as tile form.

- In addition to a large palette of standard colors, some recycled rubber can be custom colored.

CORK

Some of today's most well-heeled floors are being covered in some type of cork.

When it comes to cork, age is a good thing. The older the tree, the better the quality of cork it can produce. Approximately every ten years, the bark of the cork tree is stripped from its trunk and transformed into everything from wine stoppers to fashionable floors. (There's no harm to the tree, either, evidenced by the fact that—harvested or not—the species can live more than five hundred years.) It's the latter that's getting a lot of attention today; natural cork is not only eco-friendly but, thanks to its honeycomb structure, completely comfortable, too. For example, if you stand in the kitchen for long periods of time, a floor made of cork will be easier on the feet than one made of ceramic tile. That's not

GREEN DECORATING & REMODELING

Natural Cork

- Cork floors are nonslip and durable; they even recover well from marks left by furniture.

- Due to cork's outstanding insulation properties, it can reduce heating/cooling costs.

- Floors made of cork are anti-static and hypoallergenic. Look for those with nontoxic, water-based finishes, too.

- Cork can be used in wet areas such as kitchens and baths, but the seams of snap-lock cork flooring need to be sealed.

Cork + Color

- In addition to its traditional brown, cork is available in a wide array of colors.

- Shades range from subtle slate grays to brilliant tangerines.

- Colored cork flooring is most often found in tile form.

- Look for colors and/or finishes that are water based, a better choice than those with potentially harmful toxins.

surprising, considering that cork's content is 50 percent air. Plus cork contains a natural, wax-like substance that makes it moisture-resistant.

Part of cork's beauty lies in its versatility. It comes in rolls, planks, tiles, and even mosaics. Contrary to what you might think, however, cork flooring comes in a wide array of hues. By mixing and matching tile shapes and colors, you can create a custom, one-of-a-kind floor.

Two all-natural materials combine to form recycled rubber/cork flooring tiles. This composite material, made up of recycled rubber and mineral fillers with cork granules, is resilient, durable, and easy to maintain. Both the cork and rubber are 100 percent postproduction waste. Any waste produced in the manufacturing process is recycled back into the product.

Cork + Pattern

- Because cork flooring is produced from granules, the inherent pattern is created by the size of the granules used.

- Colored cork tiles can be arranged to form any number of patterns.

- Shapes other than square are also available; rectangles, for instance, can be used to create a herringbone pattern.

- Some patterned cork floors can even have a three-dimensional effect.

Mosaic-Style Cork

- Natural mosaic tile has the same insulating and sound-proofing qualities as other types of cork.

- Cork mosaics measure one inch in diameter and, like mosaic tile, come in sheets.

- Also, like their ceramic counterparts, cork mosaics must be grouted.

- Most mosaics can be tinted with natural wood stains.

CERAMIC TILE

The durability and design versatility of ceramic tile makes it an attractive option.

For a moment, set aside all the aesthetic advantages that ceramic tile offers; with its wide range of patterns and colors, that's a given. But there are plenty of practical benefits, too. It's durable, stain-resistant, and easy to clean.

Most tile is simply referred to as ceramic, but within that category there are several sub-types, each with its own dis-

tinct character and best uses. In addition to true ceramic tile, there's also porcelain and terra-cotta. One of the things they have in common, though, is that they come in a wide variety of colors.

Just be sure to check the slip-resistant rating on the floor tiles of your choice so they don't send you sailing. Manufac-

Ceramic

- Ceramic tile retains heat and emits it slowly, so it's especially good in climates that are warm during the day and cool at night.

- Although this material can be energy intensive to produce, it's offset by tile's durability.

- Ceramic tile is low maintenance; cleaning requires little more than a damp cloth.

- Tile's vast color palette and variety of patterns make decorative possibilities all but endless.

Porcelain

- Porcelain is harder and denser than standard ceramic because it contains less clay and more of the mineral feldspar.

- Because porcelain is denser, it's better for high-moisture areas such as bathrooms.

- Like conventional ceramic tile, porcelain is available in glazed and unglazed varieties. However, glazed tiles are easier to keep clean.

- Porcelain is highly stain- and scratch-resistant.

turers measure slip resistance in terms of a tile's Coefficient of Friction (COF). The higher the COF, the more slip-resistant the tile is. This rating is particularly important when selecting a floor tile for areas that will invariably get wet, such as the bathroom floor or the shower.

It stands to reason that unglazed tile is less slippery than glazed tile, but there's another way to add an extra element of safety. Using a smaller tile, such as 6x6-inch squares or even penny tiles, will necessitate more grout, which is a non-slip surface, too.

ZOOM

A tile floor has passive solar heating benefits, too. Ceramic tile absorbs heat well, darker tiles even more so than those that are light in color. If your new ceramic floor won't get a lot of natural light, you may want to install radiant heat beneath it to keep the surface from feeling too cool—especially on bare feet.

Terra-Cotta

- Four basic materials make up terra-cotta: clay, sand, topsoil, and water.

- Depending on the clay that's used, terra-cotta tiles can range in color from a light reddish brown to nearly black.

- In its natural state, terra-cotta has a matte finish, but it comes in colored glazes, too.

- Terra-cotta is naturally hard, as well as waterproof, making it better for high-moisture areas.

Recycled

- Recycled ceramic tile can be more durable and stain-resistant than its nonrecycled counterpart.

- The recycled content can be as much as 95 percent.

- Look for recycled ceramic tiles with glazes that have no lead or toxins.

- Reclaimed raw materials can also be used to create porcelain tiles; their recycled content is typically about 50 percent.

PLANKS AND TILES

93

CLAY TILE

The warmth of clay tile is matched only by its sturdy character.

Clay tile can add casual appeal to any room. Its naturally rustic look can be found in a variety of forms, from Saltillo tile to brick.

Because the clay is typically left outside to cure in the sun, it's not at all unusual to find animal tracks in finished Saltillo tiles. These inherent imperfections actually enhance its beauty and character—unlike glazed ceramic, where imperfections would be viewed as a defect. Some homeowners even give these tiles priority placement. A word to the wise, however: Saltillo tile is porous and can scuff or stain easily. As a result, it's extremely important to use a strong sealer.

The durability of brick is hard to beat, but to get the look

GREEN DECORATING & REMODELING

Clay

- Clay tile, made of clay, volcanic topsoil, and sand, is created by firing it at a high temperature.

- A high silica content gives clay tile even more strength and wear-resistance.

- Clay tiles come in square form as well as other shapes, including rectangles and hexagons.

- To give clay tile a "wet" look, it can be finished with a water-based acrylic seal that only needs occasional damp mopping.

Saltillo

- Mexican Saltillo tiles are formed by either pressing quarried clay into a wood frame or carving the desired shape.

- The color isn't limited to basic terra-cotta; colors such as red and black can also be found.

- Some Saltillo tiles are given a hand-rubbed finish, resulting in a more rustic look.

- Because this type of tile is very porous, it soaks up liquid easily. And be careful, it also stains and scuffs easily.

you don't need to use the real thing. The sheer weight of a brick floor is more than most rooms can handle. Brick tiles provide the same look, but because they're thinner than true brick, can be installed in the same way as standard ceramic tile. And new tiles aren't your only option. Keep an eye out for recycled brick tiles that have been salvaged from old buildings. Taking that extra green step can make a big difference for the environment.

Brick

- Generally, brick floor tiles are available in half-inch and one-inch thicknesses.

- Look for tiles that are smooth, making them easy to clean, but that still have good slip-resistance.

- Brick tile is available in a spectrum of colors, ranging from deep reds and browns to paler grays.

- You'll also find brick tile that has been salvaged from old buildings.

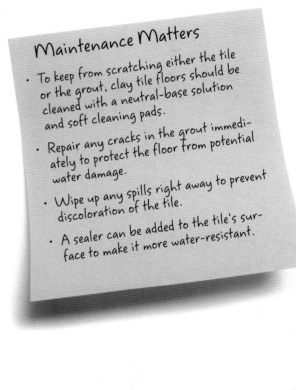

Maintenance Matters

- To keep from scratching either the tile or the grout, clay tile floors should be cleaned with a neutral-base solution and soft cleaning pads.

- Repair any cracks in the grout immediately to protect the floor from potential water damage.

- Wipe up any spills right away to prevent discoloration of the tile.

- A sealer can be added to the tile's surface to make it more water-resistant.

PLANKS AND TILES

GLASS TILE

Today's innovations in glass tile are reinventing this timeless material, making it more green.

As green consciousness continues to be raised, more home-owners are looking to glass tile for their floors. Available in conventional sizes as well as mosaic shapes, in brand-new varieties as well as recycled, this time-tested material is being discovered all over again.

At first, glass tile may not be an obvious choice for floors, because it's naturally shiny and slick. But an increasing number of manufacturers are now producing slip-resistant options. Available in larger tiles as well as mosaics, glass is completely non-toxic. Just be sure that the grout and adhesives you use are free of harmful chemicals, too.

Likewise, there's a wealth of recycled glass tiles available to-

GREEN DECORATING & REMODELING

Glass Tile

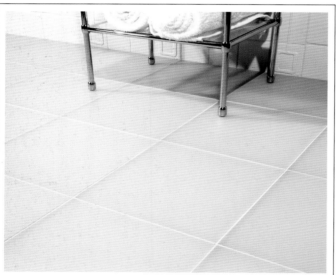

- Some glass tiles are fused, which requires less energy in the production process than conventional melting.

- Available in a vast array of colors, glass tile has a translucent and iridescent quality.

- Glass is impervious to moisture, making it a particularly good choice for kitchens and baths.

- Glass tile is not only durable but also easy to clean.

Glass Mosaics

- Due to the high compressive strength of glass, mosaics made of the material are a good choice for floors.

- Glass mosaics come in a wide variety of colors and textures.

- Glass tile reflects light, creating a shimmering surface.

- Glass mosaics allow for almost limitless possibilities in terms of pattern.

day. Once you start seeking them out, you'll realize just how creative this type of flooring can be. In addition to tiles that look just like virgin glass, recycled content is being mixed with other materials to create a wide variety of looks. You will find floor tiles that have the appearance of ceramic, porcelain, and even stone, all made up of at least 50 percent recycled glass. No one will be the wiser that these green options are anything other than the real thing!

Recycled Glass Tile

More Recycled Glass Forms

- Recycled glass tiles can contain up to 100 percent recycled content.

- The amount of recycled content in a tile can vary greatly by its color; manufacturers can provide specific percentages.

- Glass is recycled from various sources. For instance, some tiless are the result of recycled window glass mixed with metallic oxides.

- Some contain recycled green and brown bottles, which are typically the most difficult types of glass to find new uses for.

- Some tiles today are using recycled glass to create a variety of distinctive looks.

- With 55 percent recycled glass in the product, these tiles can effect the appearance of everything from porcelain to metal.

- These tiles can be SCS (Scientific Certification Systems) certified.

- Complementary wall tiles are also available, some of them are even embossed.

CORK

Though relatively new on the flooring scene, cork is an earth-friendly choice.

Think beyond the material you remember as the quintessential schoolroom tack surface. Today's cork is one of the most eco-friendly flooring options you'll find. Available in both tile and plank forms, cork regenerates quickly, which qualifies it as a rapidly renewable resource. It's easy to install, and has health benefits, too. The material is both hypoallergenic (resists mold and mildew) and antistatic (doesn't attract dust or pollen).

Cork tiles make it possible to create any number of floor configurations. By combining two or more colors (and, yes, cork comes in more than basic brown), you can create everything from a simple checkerboard pattern to an intricate inlaid

Glue-Down Tiles

- These types of cork tiles are available in a wide array of shapes and colors, allowing you to create unlimited designs.

- Inlay borders are now being offered, ranging from simple diamond patterns to Southwest-inspired bands.

- Easy for the do-it-yourselfer to install, glue-down cork tiles are also less costly per square inch than their floating plank counterparts.

- They can be used in practically any space, including potentially wet areas like the kitchen and bath.

Floating Tiles

- Floating cork tiles can be applied on top of almost any surface (with the exception of carpet) as long as the subfloor is level and dry.

- Planks come in just as many colors as glue-down tiles.

- A glueless, snap-lock system makes this type of tile easy to install.

- Like glue-down tiles, these 12x12-inch squares can be configured in any number of ways.

design. Or, you may decide that all the pattern you need is within the cork itself. Depending upon how the tiles are made, the surface can have an all-over granular pattern or an irregular textured look.

Cork planks, on the other hand, have a more consistent overall pattern. As a result, they can deceptively look like a hardwood floor. The only similarity between cork and hardwood, though, is in the way it's cared for. All it needs is to be vacuumed or damp mopped on a regular basis.

Floating Planks

- Individual cork planks typically measure 1x3 feet.

- Like floating cork tiles, this option has a glueless, snap-lock system that makes it easy to install.

- This kind of floating system provides maximum comfort and noise absorption.

- Floating cork plank floors can be installed over radiant heat systems, although cork is a good insulator on its own.

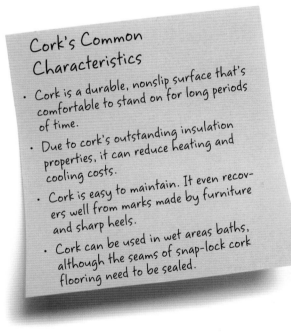

Cork's Common Characteristics

- Cork is a durable, nonslip surface that's comfortable to stand on for long periods of time.

- Due to cork's outstanding insulation properties, it can reduce heating and cooling costs.

- Cork is easy to maintain. It even recovers well from marks made by furniture and sharp heels.

- Cork can be used in wet areas baths, although the seams of snap-lock cork flooring need to be sealed.

PLANKS AND TILES

99

STONE

Natural stone floors are incredibly durable, which is one of their most eco-friendly assets.

On the surface, natural stone floors may not seem to be the most eco-friendly option, but if you look deeper you'll find that their durability alone makes them a prime contender. Marble, granite, slate, and travertine are just a few of the stone possibilities, each one with its own singular style.

With its wide array of colors and inherent veining, marble tile makes a striking floor covering. Because it's expensive, however, marble is usually reserved for small spaces like baths.

Granite is on the high end of the cost spectrum, too, but—unlike marble—it's scratch-resistant, making it suitable for more applications. Granite can stand up to a high-traffic area like the kitchen and is waterproof, too. Meanwhile, terrazzo

GREEN DECORATING & REMODELING

Marble

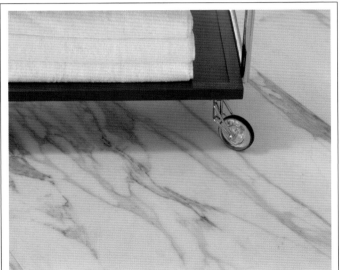

- Marble, due to its expense alone, is typically reserved for smaller spaces such as bathrooms.

- Polished marble is waterproof and heatproof, but requires occasional resealing.

- Because marble is not as hard as granite, it's more susceptible to household acids, such as nail polish remover, which will remove a finish.

- Polished marble scratches more easily than granite; honed marble shows wear less readily.

Granite

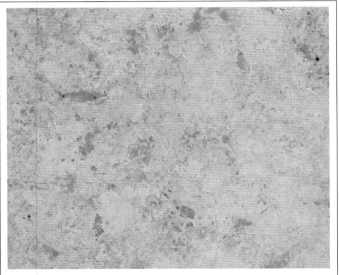

- Granite floors require periodic sealing; use a low-VOC (volatile organic compound) sealant, if possible.

- Granite can also be honed (unpolished), but the resulting matte surface is more prone to stain.

- Left unsealed, granite will absorb stains such as oil, which can ultimately cause discoloration.

- Sharp blows can cause granite to chip or crack.

fuses these two types of stone. This flooring is a mix of marble, granite, onyx, and/or glass chips, with cement acting as the binder. It can either be precast or poured in place, but either way, terrazzo's polished surface is perfectly suited for floors.

Like granite, slate is water-resistant and will stand up to heavy foot traffic. It's also a less expensive option. And if you think all slate is the color of chalkboards, think again. It varies from pitch black to beige and many shades in between. Travertine, meanwhile, is much more porous, and needs to be sealed. Use a no- or low-VOC sealer that's slip-resistant.

Slate

- Tumbled slate is a better option for floors than clefted slate; it is more slip-resistant and easier on bare feet.

- Stone tile, such as slate, serves as a type of passive solar heating. It holds and radiates heat long after the sun goes down.

- To make slate more stain-resistant, finish it with an appropriate sealer.

- Look for slate, or any stone tile, from local quarries.

Travertine

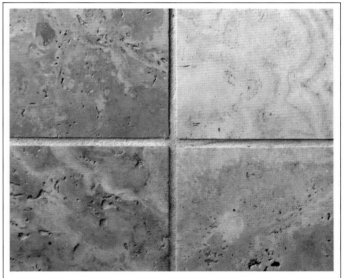

- Travertine, beyond its inherent beauty, has the durability of any natural stone.

- This stone comes in a variety of colors, ranging from soft white to a rich mahogany.

- Travertine's colors blend to create a distinct pattern.

- In addition to conventional tile, travertine moldings are also available.

PLANKS AND TILES

CREATIVE TILE IDEAS

Today's inventive tile options are enough to stimulate anyone's creative spirit.

The materials used to create today's floor tiles are everything you can imagine and more. Carpet tiles, for instance, have made great strides, in both appearance and application. You'll find a wide assortment of low-VOC tiles, including some made of natural fibers such as hemp and wool. Not only are they simple to install—creating a wall-to-wall carpet, an area rug, or hall runner—they're typically just as easy to peel up and take with you when you move. Some manufacturers have even gone the extra mile to think about how to dispose of their products; all the consumer has to do is to call for recycling instructions.

Likewise, metals such as aluminum and brass are being

Carpet

- Carpet tiles are readily available today, some of which are made of natural fibers such as wool and hemp.

- The backings of the carpet tiles are a composite, made up of some recycled items.

- These tiles come in a wide assortment of colors and patterns, making it easy to create one-of-a-kind rugs of any size.

- Carpet tiles like these are recyclable, too.

Metal

- Metal tiles can be found in a wide variety of materials, from brass and bronze to aluminum and stainless steel.

- Like almost all other tiles, metal types come in finishes ranging from matte to glossy.

- Metal tiles can be installed edge to edge. When little or no grout is used, the likelihood of VOC emissions is reduced.

- Some metal tiles contain up to 100 percent recycled content by using reclaimed materials such as aluminum and brass.

recycled for use as floor tiles. These tiles typically range in size from 2x2 inches up to 12x12 inches. As a general rule, though, larger tiles are better suited for floor use. Not only do they require less adhesive and grout, but because there aren't so many grout lines to visually break up the flooring, they also create a more expansive-looking surface.

Floor tiles are even being made from recycled sources such as leather and rubber tiles. As manufacturers get more creative, you can too.

Leather

- Recycled leather floor tiles provide the look of genuine leather at a more budget-friendly price.

- Look for tiles made of 100 percent recycled leather.

- Like the real thing, recycled leather tiles vary in grain, texture, and color.

- Like other absorbent natural materials, a floor covered in recycled leather tiles requires the appropriate sealer. Check with your local retailer.

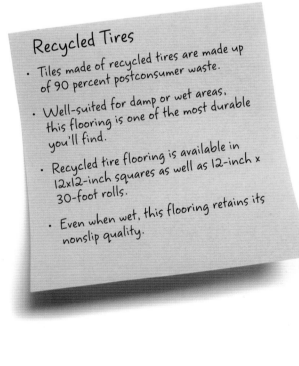

Recycled Tires

- Tiles made of recycled tires are made up of 90 percent postconsumer waste.

- Well-suited for damp or wet areas, this flooring is one of the most durable you'll find.

- Recycled tire flooring is available in 12x12-inch squares as well as 12-inch x 30-foot rolls.

- Even when wet, this flooring retains its nonslip quality.

STONE

Countertops made of stone are not only durable, they're infinitely recyclable, too.

Countertops serve two purposes. First, they provide a safe and solid surface on which to prepare meals, and second, they look good in the process. Natural stone isn't a renewable resource, but its durability makes it a good long-term choice, one that won't readily be discarded. Plus, its natural colors and textures are appealing, too.

Granite is a dense material and, as a result, hard to scratch. It's stain-resistant, but not impervious, either, especially to oil. By sealing the surface periodically, you can keep those stains at bay. As for marble, much of its beauty lies in its veining. And no two pieces are alike, assuring you a one-of-a-kind look. It does scratch easily, however, and is susceptible to acids, such as

GREEN DECORATING & REMODELING

Granite

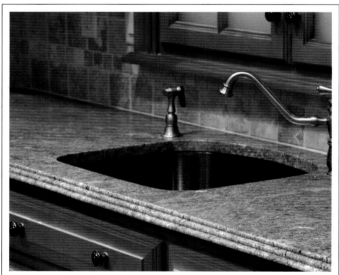

- Because granite is a very hard stone, it's not susceptible to heat.

- Left unsealed, granite will absorb stains such as oil, which can ultimately cause discoloration.

- Granite countertops can also be honed (unpolished), but the resulting matte surface is more prone to stains.

- Sharp blows can cause granite to chip or crack.

Marble

- Polished marble is waterproof and heat-proof, but requires occasional resealing.

- Because marble is not as hard as granite, it's more susceptible to acids such as mustard, ketchup, and vinegar, which will remove a polished finish.

- Polished marble scratches more easily than granite; honed marble shows wear less readily.

lemon juice. Many people like the way that marble shows these "wear marks" over time. If you're looking for a countertop that's always pristine, however, marble may not be your best choice.

Limestone and slate are readily available resources for countertops, plus soapstone and volcanic lava can be used for this purpose, too. Soapstone, which is relatively stain-resistant, has a smooth surface and a dark gray color that usually deepens over time. Volcanic lava, available in a variety of colors, can be fired to produce finishes from matte to high-gloss. Whichever stone you choose, use sealers and cleaners specific to the material.

········· GREEN ● LIGHT ··············

Search out local salvage stores for slabs of natural stone that you can reconfigure for your own countertop. And think outside the box, too. If you can't find pieces large enough to create a continuous surface, select smaller ones that can be cut into tiles.

Limestone

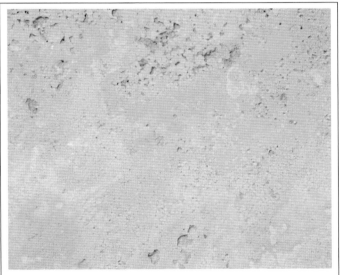

- Limestone comes in a wide variety of colors, but the majority of the pieces you'll see have lighter tones.

- Because this material is porous, it needs to be sealed adequately.

- Some types of limestone are more dense, and thus harder, than others.

- It's common for limestone to have natural imprints, left by shells and fossils, for instance, making each piece one-of-a-kind.

Slate

- Slate countertops range in color from charcoal gray and black to deep reds and greens.

- Although it's a hard stone, this type of surface has a smooth, velvety feeling.

- This type of stone warms up with the sun's rays, providing passive solar heating.

- Slate needs to be sealed to make it more stain-resistant.

TILE

The design versatility of tile makes it an attractive option for countertops throughout the house.

Tile not only provides a hard-as-nails working surface, but countertops made of this material can be customized with color and pattern to your heart's content. As is the case with many products, however, there are certain trade-offs. Ceramic tile, for instance, is typically glazed with toxic chemicals. On the other hand, it's durable and can be recycled, too, even if it's a matter of breaking the tiles down to make a mosaic-topped table. Porcelain has many of the same properties as ceramic tile; the only real differences are that porcelain is harder and comes in more limited colors and patterns.

Glass tile has a shiny surface similar to that of ceramic. Its trans-

Ceramic

- Ceramic tile is a relatively inexpensive choice for countertops, available in virtually every color, pattern, and texture.

- Its durable and easy-to-clean qualities make ceramic tile an even more attractive choice. Ceramic tile is heat-resistant, too.

- Tiles can be prone to chip or crack, and grout can become stained if not properly sealed.

- Look for ceramic tile made from recycled content such as old light bulbs, bottles, and porcelain.

Glass

- Glass tiles that are appropriate for countertops come in a wide variety of colors. However, textures and patterns are more limited.

- Like ceramic, glass is durable but can chip or crack if something heavy is dropped on it.

- Glass is easy to clean and heat-resistant.

- Some glass tile is recycled, and all glass tile can be recycled again.

lucency, though, is more reflective, so a room that gets even a little natural light will seem brighter, too. Plus, glass tile is stain-resistant, a big plus for kitchen or bath countertops. If it's an earthier look you want, consider terra-cotta tiles. Their natural reddish brown color adds visual warmth and even those glazed with color have warm undertones. Whether your preference is rustic or refined, there's a type of tile to suit your sense of style.

ZOOM

If you like the look of natural stone, but not the price tag that comes with stone slabs, consider incorporating stone tiles instead. All of the options that are available in slab form, from marble and granite to slate and limestone, can be cut into thin squares.

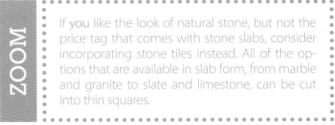

Porcelain

- Porcelain is denser and harder than standard ceramic, making it a good choice for kitchen countertops.

- This material doesn't absorb water or smells, making it particularly good for bathrooms and kitchens.

- Like conventional ceramic tile, porcelain is available in glazed and unglazed varieties; glazed is easier to keep clean.

- Porcelain is both stain- and scratch-resistant.

Terra-Cotta

- In their natural state, terra-cotta tiles can range in color from a light reddish brown to nearly black depending on the clay used to create it.

- Terra-cotta can be given colorful, glazed finishes, too.

- Terra-cotta is naturally hard as well as waterproof.

- Hand-molded terra-cotta tiles can contain up to 50 percent postconsumer and postindustrial recycled content.

COUNTERTOPS

SOLID SURFACES

In solid-surface countertops, eco-friendly and recycled elements are adding up to substantial style.

Solid-surface countertops have just that going for them— solidity. Because these custom-cut options are installed in a single piece, scratches can typically be sanded out. Plus, they're stain-resistant and their seamless quality means fewer crevices for crumbs to get caught in.

An increasingly popular option is also one that may seem the least likely: countertops created from paper. Layers of kraft paper are held together by resin, creating a countertop that's between one quarter and two inches thick. Standard paperstone countertops are readily available, but the more green option is one made from recycled paper that uses nontoxic resin, too. Likewise, shimmering glass tiles can be used to construct

Recycled Paper

- Composite paperstone that's constructed from recycled paper and bonded with a water-based resin is the most eco-friendly.

- Paperstone is durable and scratch-resistant as well as stain- and heat-resistant.

- This type of paperstone, made with 100 percent post-consumer recycled paper can be FSC certified.

Glass

- Conducive to creating countertops, 100 percent recycled glass is available in cut sheets.

- The color of the glass surface is dependent on its contents. Color options include blue, green, white, and brown.

- This type of countertop can be cleaned like any other piece of glass.

- Perhaps surprisingly, this material is also well suited for flooring applications.

a countertop. Recycled glass tiles are available, too, and some recycled glass even comes in sheet form. The latter has the advantage not only from a green point of view, but it doesn't require grout, which has the potential to offgas VOCs (volatile organic compounds).

You'll also find alternatives to natural stone. Composites, for instance, have a texture that's similar to limestone and soapstone but are primarily made of paper and glass. And engineered stone is made of quartz, one of the hardest materials you'll find. Any of these surfaces can be a good choice.

Composites

- Composite countertops are made up of a mix a materials—recycled paper, recycled glass, coal fly ash, and Portland cement.

- An alternative to natural stone, composite countertops are hand cast into slabs that resemble soapstone or limestone.

- This type of countertop comes in limited colors.

- To maintain its surface, this material should be refinished on a regular basis.

Engineered Stone

- Engineered stone countertops are made primarily of quartz, one of nature's hardest materials.

- The nonporous surface resists scratches; it's also stain- and acid-resistant.

- This material is available in a wide range of colors, though the necessary color pigments and resins are typically less than eco-friendly.

- Engineered stone, which doesn't require sealing, is easy to clean, too.

CONCRETE

More people are opting for concrete, one of the most durable countertop materials you'll find.

It's not just for your basement floor anymore. Concrete has worked its way up, now appearing in the form of fashionable countertops. They can be precast to fit your space or created on-site, left in their traditional gray hue or given a color stain. Who knew that a substance consisting of cement, sand, and stone could be so cutting-edge?

Concrete, in its pure form, can provide an industrial-strength countertop. But therein lies ones of its drawbacks, too. It's an extremely heavy material that, before you get serious about installing, requires adequate support. Keep in mind, too, that it's a porous material and, even with regular waxing or sealing, it can stain and—over time—develop hairline cracks. That said,

The Pure Form

- Concrete countertops can be made to look like virtually any material, from tile and brick to slate and wood.

- Countertops made of concrete are durable, economical, and easy to maintain.

- The material can be stained and sealed or left untreated. Both acid stains and water-based stains are available.

- Concrete is heat- and scratch-resistant but can be costly, too.

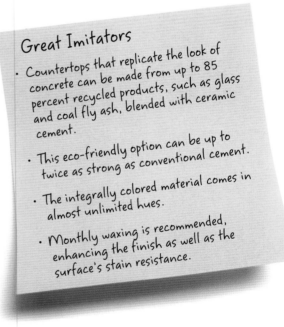

Great Imitators

- Countertops that replicate the look of concrete can be made from up to 85 percent recycled products, such as glass and coal fly ash, blended with ceramic cement.

- This eco-friendly option can be up to twice as strong as conventional cement.

- The integrally colored material comes in almost unlimited hues.

- Monthly waxing is recommended, enhancing the finish as well as the surface's stain resistance.

it can be customized to virtually any size and shape you can imagine.

As the popularity of concrete continues to grow, you'll also find alternatives that offer the same look in more eco-friendly ways. There are materials that replicate the look of concrete that are made from up to 85 percent recycled products, as well as an option made primarily of cellulose fibers that's twice as strong as cement. Even composites that combine concrete and recycled glass have come into the picture; their sparkling shards of imbedded glass add a touch of color, too.

ZOOM

Made from cement and recycled materials such as plastic water bottles, postconsumer glass, postindustrial metal shavings, and rubber tires, Syndecrete is a solid surface material with twice the strength and half the weight of concrete. Offered in solid and aggregate colors, it not only comes in precast slabs but also in tiles, sinks, and tabletops.

Cellulose

- Another eco-friendly alternative to traditional concrete is Eco-Cem®, which includes a high percentage of cellulose fibers.

- This material will develop a patina over time.

- Because the surface is prone to staining, spills should be cleaned up immediately.

- Eco-Cem panels can also be used for walls and floors.

Concrete-and-Glass Composites

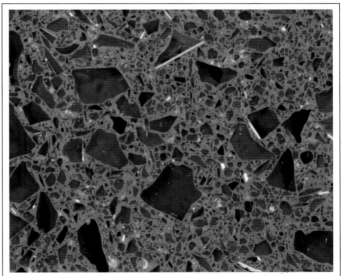

- Terrazo-like composites made of recycled glass and concrete have the durability of granite, are not as porous as marble, and are heat-resistant like stone.

- The wide variety of colors depend on the size and color of the recycled glass within.

- The material is VOC free and the chemical composition is benign and 99.5 percent inorganic. It is very safe in terms of toxicity and fire resistance.

- This type of material is recyclable and can be cut into smaller pieces such as tiles and tabletops.

COUNTERTOPS

WOOD

To add warmth to a kitchen countertop, the look of wood is hard to beat.

Wood has a warm and luminous appeal for countertops and kitchens with oak, maple, cherry, red beech, walnut, teak, and mahogany all favored for countertops. Wood is one of the more sanitary products for the kitchen, too, with inherent properties to protect it from bacteria buildup. Maintenance is required, however, starting with regular mineral oil treatments, particularly near the sink, and extra caution with extremely hot cookware. Wood countertops have a green advantage in that the material is a renewable resource. But, to take the eco-friendly concept a step further, consider

Natural

- Wood countertops are available in a wide variety of colors and finishes.

- This material can be damaged by water and stains over time but can be sanded and resealed as necessary.

- Look for wood with FSC certification; use low-VOC sealers and water-based finishes.

- Countertops that highlight the wood's natural edge are appropriate for small spaces, such as bathroom vanities.

Butcher Block

Butcher block countertops generally vary in thickness between 1¼ and 6 inches.

- Butcher block is a slab surface, much in the same way as granite.

- Maple has long been the wood of choice for butcher block, but you'll also find walnut, cherry, oak, teak, and lyptus—which is both affordable and renewable.

- Most butcher block surfaces can be cleaned with just soap and water. If the wood has a mineral oil finish, it will need to be re-oiled regularly.

- Oil-finished butcher block can be used as a cutting surface.

having a countertop crafted of Forest Stewardship Council (FSC)–certified wood or even from salvaged lumber.

Butcher block, meanwhile, has been used for years for specialty surfaces, such as cutting boards. But people are realizing that this surface, most often made of stacked and glued pieces of hard maple, can be just as suitable throughout a kitchen. The thing to remember, however, is that butcher block is prone to water damage, so it shouldn't be positioned near a sink unless it's well sealed.

You can even get the look of wood with an entirely different material. Bamboo, one of the most rapidly renewable resources, lends the same warmth that you'll find in wood countertops. And this giant grass is durable, too. Take a look in your local housewares store and you'll see that bamboo is even going head-to-head with butcher block as a sturdy cutting surface. Whether you opt for this up-and-comer or the real thing, you can breathe easier knowing that, ultimately, all of these surfaces are recyclable, too.

Bamboo

- Ranging from pale yellow to rich honeyed hues, bamboo countertops can have a vertical grain or be done in parquet style.

- Although bamboo is a grass, countertops made of the material are harder than maple wood.

- Look for bamboo countertops with nontoxic, formaldehyde-free adhesives.

- Bamboo can be sealed with mineral oil or, as a more natural option, walnut oil followed by a coat of beeswax.

Reclaimed Wood

- Certain reclaimed woods can be transformed into countertops, including heart pine, oak, and chestnut.

- Salvaged wood can come from any number of sources, from abandoned buildings to pilings and barges.

- In addition to this type of wood being green, it adds instant character to a room.

- Companies that sell reclaimed wood sometimes also offer architectural salvage such as doors and windows, too.

METAL

Countertops crafted of metal are finding their way from commercial kitchens to the home.

It's no coincidence that stainless steel is the surface of choice for restaurateurs. This countertop material is non-porous, which limits bacteria growth, and it doesn't chip. In fact, it's practically indestructible. While it's true that stainless steel can be noisier than, for example, countertops made of wood, and it can have a tendency to show fingerprints, this type of metal is a solid choice from a green point of view because it's entirely recyclable. If you're a devotee of the industrial look, look for stainless steel pieces, such as work tables, at restaurant-supply companies. Better yet, keep an eye out for soon-to-be discarded pieces if you know of a restaurant about to be remodeled.

Stainless Steel

- Stainless steel countertops lend a contemporary and, to some degree, industrial look.

- This metal scratches easily but is easy to clean, durable, and heat-resistant.

- Stainless steel can be an expensive choice, even in the same range as natural stone.

- Look for salvaged metal or steel with a high percentage of recycled content.

Copper

- Copper, a pliable material, can be used for countertops with a warm, shiny surface.

- Hammered and smooth finishes are available; even finishing touches, such as bull-nose edges, can be formed with copper.

- The natural color of copper can be maintained with a special cleaner or left to oxidize naturally.

- Copper is a naturally self-renewing surface that's hygienic, too.

Copper and zinc are good candidates for countertops, too. Like stainless steel, they're recyclable and don't require more than soap and water to clean. Copper surfaces lend a warm glow that's all but unmatched. Zinc, on the other hand, can either be polished to look like stainless steel or allowed to age naturally to a cool gray blue hue. Keep in mind, however, that zinc can be susceptible to staining.

The types of metal showing up on counters continue to expand. And why not? In the kitchen, especially, it's a distinct advantage that they are heatproof. Lead-free pewter has a luxurious look, eventually taking on a charcoal gray patina. More rare, but still suitable, are bronze, a combination of copper and tin, and brass, a combination of copper and zinc. The mix of metals makes both alloys harder than copper. Likewise, both bronze and brass take on a dark brownish black patina over time.

If there's a downside, it's that all metals have a tendency to scratch; keep the cutting board close at hand and consider any stray marks just part of the charm.

Zinc

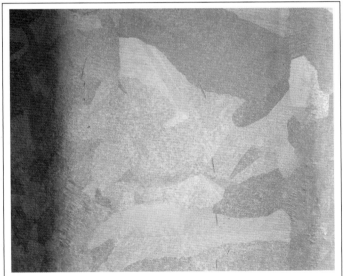

- Zinc, in its polished state, is similar in appearance to stainless steel or aluminum.

- Countertops made of zinc can be maintained with special cleaners or left to oxidize naturally to a deep blue gray.

- Zinc countertops can be cleaned on a daily basis with just soap and water.

- Like all metals, zinc is susceptible to scratches, but they can typically be rubbed out.

Recycled Aluminum

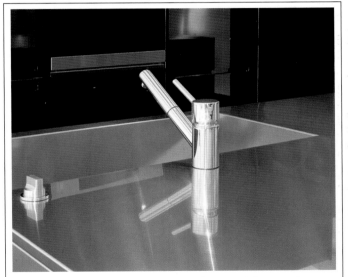

- Countertops made of recycled aluminum are durable and heat-resistant.

- Look for countertops that have nonreactive, nontoxic clear finishes.

- Like its stainless steel counterpart, this kind of finish doesn't leave fingerprints.

- Aluminum isn't cold to the touch; its highly conductive nature keeps it at room temperature.

REFRIGERATORS

Today's energy-efficient refrigerators conserve natural resources and save you money, too.

The refrigerators you'll find today are much more efficient that those of the past, thanks in large part to the fact that Freon—a refrigerant known to burn holes in the ozone—has finally been phased out. Some of the best offerings are Energy Star models, which use approximately 15 percent less energy than current federal standards mandate. That trans-

lates to refrigerators that are 40 percent more efficient than conventional models built before 2001, and 50 percent more efficient than those built before 1993.

The efficiency of a refrigerator depends on the style that you select. As a general rule, top- and bottom-freezer models not only cost less than their side-by-side counterparts, they

Energy Star Refrigerators

- Refrigerators with Energy Star status feature high-efficiency compressors and insulation, as well as precise temperature and defrost mechanisms.

- These models use at least 15 percent less energy than required by current federal standards.

- Qualified models are also available with top, bottom, and side-by-side freezers. Many include automatic ice makers and ice dispensers.

- Replacing an old refrigerator with an Energy Star model saves enough energy to light the average house for four months.

Top- and Bottom-Freezer Refrigerators

- While top- and bottom-freezer refrigerators are more efficient than side-by-side models, bottom-freezer versions are slightly more energy efficient.

- Bottom-freezer models allow a clear view of the contents, letting you get what you need quickly.

- Top- and bottom-freezer refrigerators have wider shelves, which accommodate oversize items more easily than side-by-side models.

- Forgoing an ice maker or door dispenser in any model can result in energy savings up to 20 percent.

also tend to use less energy, saving approximately five to twenty dollars per year in electricity costs. Be sure, as well, to choose a size that best meets your needs; the smaller the refrigerator, the more energy efficient it will be. Fewer features, such as ice makers, make a refrigerator more energy efficient and space efficient, as they don't take up any storage space.

Refrigerators produce a certain amount of heat. Position yours in a well-ventilated place, keeping excess heat from getting trapped, which requires extra air conditioning.

········· GREEN ● LIGHT ···············

Before getting rid of any old appliance, check with your electric company to see if a bounty program is offered in your area. If not, contact your municipal department of public works to inquire about the procedures for collecting and disposing of appliances. Turn to the resources section (page 238) to find more information on recycling options.

Compact Refrigerators

- The smaller the size of your refrigerator, the more efficient it will be.

- Compact refrigerators are well suited for everywhere from game rooms to dorm rooms, home offices to efficiency apartments.

- Energy Star versions are also available in these smaller sizes.

- A space-saving refrigerator/freezer/microwave operates on a single plug, using about half the electricity that two separately plugged-in appliances would.

Drawer-Style Refrigerators

- Drawer-style refrigerators can't take the place of conventional models in the kitchen, but they are handy for storing snacks and keeping items at different temperatures.

- Because the units are small in size, they also lose less cold air when opened.

- With a capacity of about four cubic feet, these drawers fit into standard cabinets.

- Avoid placing refrigerator drawers next to the oven or dishwasher, as the added heat makes the units work harder.

STOVES

Regardless of your personal taste and style, any stove can be green to some degree.

Long gone are the days when all stoves were created equal. Thanks to innovations in kitchen appliances, there's a wide variety of eco-friendly stoves—as well as separate ovens and cooktops—from which to choose. In the past, gas cooktops had the advantage over electric models if for no other reason than their instant on/instant off capability resulted in shorter cooking times. Gas is still a good option, but now there's an energy-efficient electric alternative, too. The burners of induction cooktops transfer electromagnetic energy directly to the pan, leaving the burners themselves relatively cool. At the same time, food can be heated to a precise temperature 50 percent faster than on any other gas or electric model.

Gas Stoves

- The instant on/instant off capability of gas keeps cooking times to a minimum.

- The gas flame can easily be controlled to produce as much, or as little, heat as needed.

- Gas stoves with electronic ignition use about 30 percent less energy than older models fitted with a pilot light.

- Because natural gas can release some combustion pollutants into your house, a good downdraft ventilation system is necessary.

Induction Cooktops

- In magnetic induction, the heat bypasses the burner and goes straight to the pot instead, keeping the burner relatively cool.

- Food is heated more quickly—up to 50 percent faster than conventional surfaces—and to precise temperatures.

- While induction cooktops outperform many other models, they are more expensive, too.

- Only metallic cookware such as stainless steel or cast iron will work on an induction cooktop.

Another one of the most recent advancements is the convection oven. Unlike their conventional counterparts, which allow hot air to circulate randomly, convection ovens can hold a uniform temperature, which results in faster cooking times at lower temperatures. Some consumers, in fact, find the best of both worlds in dual fuel stoves, which have gas cooktops and convection ovens.

Last but not least, the microwave oven is eco-friendly, too. It vastly shortens cooking times, which saves energy.

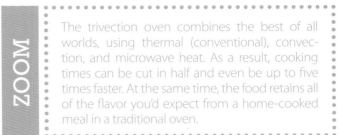

ZOOM

The trivection oven combines the best of all worlds, using thermal (conventional), convection, and microwave heat. As a result, cooking times can be cut in half and even be up to five times faster. At the same time, the food retains all of the flavor you'd expect from a home-cooked meal in a traditional oven.

Convection Ovens

- Because they cook quicker and at lower temperatures, convection ovens are more energy efficient than their conventional counterparts.

- Convection ovens are typically larger and more expensive than standard ovens.

- The uniform flow of hot air results in even cooking, no matter which rack you use.

- Combination microwave-convection ovens allow you to use the two technologies individually or together; used together, for instance, roasts come out juicier.

Microwave Ovens

- Microwave ovens use approximately 50 percent less energy than conventional ovens, and the energy that is used heats only the food and not the entire oven.

- Because no preheating is required, you save both time and energy—and the kitchen stays cooler.

- A single dish can be used for cooking and serving, reducing the amount of dishes that need to be washed.

- As a safety precaution against leakage of radioactive waves, don't stand in front of the oven while it's operating.

DISHWASHERS
Choosing the right dishwasher can go a long way toward making your kitchen green.

When shopping for an eco-friendly dishwasher, there are two points to consider: water efficiency and energy efficiency.

Most dishwashers are up to the task when it comes to cleaning dishes. Where they differ, though, is in how much water it takes to do the job well; it can vary anywhere from 3½ to 12 gallons per load. If you run your dishwasher every other day, that difference in water output alone can add up to a whopping 1,500 gallons.

Then, too, there's the matter of energy efficiency. As much as 80 percent of the energy needed to run a dishwasher is used in heating the water. On any dishwasher, be sure to check for its EnergyGuide numbers, which disclose the ap-

Water-Efficient Dishwashers

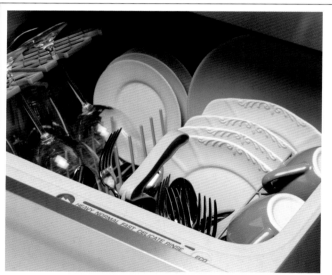

- The most water-efficient dishwashers use only about 4 gallons per wash.

- Some machines have a scanning technology that determines how soiled the water is, then decides whether a fresh-water refill is necessary.

- It takes a lot of energy consumed is used to heat the water, so water-efficient dishwashers are also energy efficient.

- Save more energy by air drying your dishes. If there isn't an air-dry switch, turn off the machine after the final rinse and open the door.

Energy-Efficient Dishwashers

- When shopping for a new dishwasher, read the EnergyGuide tag to find out how much energy (including water heating) a model is likely to use.

- Look, too, for dishwashers that are Energy Star quali-fied.

- Dishwashers with Energy Star status use at least 41 percent less energy than the federal minimum standard.

- Because it uses less hot water, an Energy Star–qualified dishwasher will save approximately ninety dollars over its lifetime.

pliance's approximate annual energy consumption. Most modern dishwashers have booster heaters that further raise the temperature of the water coming from your home's water tank. If that seems redundant, consider this: Turning the water tank's thermostat down to 120 degrees can add up to even more energy savings without compromising on cleanliness.

Finally, consider how much dishwasher you and your family really need. Most of the dishwashers sold today are built-in models that fit into a 24-inch space under a countertop.

But there are also compact models that will fit into narrower spaces and even drawer styles. If you're on the fence—sometimes you have a full load of dishes and sometimes you don't—look for a dishwasher with a half-load option, which allows you to use only the upper or lower rack.

Electric dishwashers typically use less hot water than washing and rinsing dishes by hand.

Drawer-Style Dishwashers

- Both single- and double-drawer dishwashers are available; the latter provides about the same amount of space as conventional machines.

- In double-drawer machines, the units can be used independently when you have only for a small load.

- Even when both units operate at the same time, they can be adjusted to different settings—one on "light" and one on "pots and pans," for instance.

- The drawers can be faced to match your cabinetry.

Make Dishwashing More Efficient

- Don't pre-rinse dishes before loading. You'll save nearly 20 gallons of water per load, which adds up to approximately 6,500 gallons per year.

- Avoid running the machine with anything less than a full load.

- Place large items at the sides and back of the bottom rack so they don't stop the spray from reaching the detergent dispenser.

- Avoid using special cycles. The three basic cycles—light, normal, and pots and pans—are sufficient for most loads.

121

WASHING MACHINES

An energy-efficient washer can add up to significant savings, literally and from a green point of view.

The washing machine uses more water than any other appliance in the house, so it's particularly important to make sure that it's eco-friendly.

For starters, consider a front-loading machine instead of its top-loading counterpart. Front-loading units not only accommodate more clothes per load but also use between a third to half the energy and water as those that load from the top. And, because they remove more water during the spin cycle, too, you'll use less energy drying your clothes, which adds up to savings on water and water-heating bills. Plus, front-loading machines need only a third as much detergent per load.

Front-Loading Machines

- Because a front-loading machine has no central agitator, it can hold up to 30 percent more clothing than a top-loading washer, which translates to less water usage and lower bills.

- A front-loading washer is gentler on clothes, making them last longer.

- Top-loading machines use less water and, therefore, require less detergent.

- Many front-loading machines remove more water during the spin cycle than their top-loading counterparts, which translates into shorter drying times.

Water-Efficient Machines

- Energy Star-rated washers use 18 to 20 gallons per load compared to the 40 gallons typically used by a standard washer.

- Both top- and front-loading machines can have Energy Star designations.

- Some machines are outfitted with sensors that automatically determine the water level and wash time based on the weight and size of each load.

- To be most efficient with water, run only full loads.

Front-loading washers typically do cost more, but don't make your decision based on the price of the model alone. You can save approximately $120 per year in utilities, which will add up to $1,560 over the average thirteen-year lifespan of a washer. Plus, some municipalities will make it worth your while to opt for energy-saving appliances, offering rebates for the purchase and installation of qualified energy- and water-saving machines. Certain cities even use a sliding scale: The more energy and/or water you save, the higher the rebate.

Among the options, you'll find more "intelligent washers," machines that decide how much water is needed, what temperature should be used, even the cycle best suited for the load. Because these appliances are most efficient in how much water and energy they use, many—like some of the best conventional machines—are Energy Star qualified.

The right washing machine is important, but you may need to change the way you do laundry, too. Because 80 to 85 percent of the energy used for washing clothes goes for heating the water, opt for cold water the majority of the time. While you're at it, why not use an eco-friendly detergent, too?

Energy-Efficient Machines

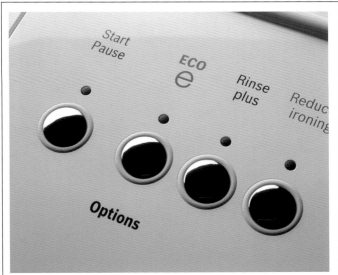

- Compared to washing machines made before 1994, Energy Star models can save up to $100 or more per year on utility bills.

- Machines with this designation use approximately 50 percent less energy than standard washers.

- Energy Star washers extract more water from clothes during the spin cycle, reducing drying time.

- You can save energy using any machine by simply using cold water for all but the toughest stains.

Intelligent Washers

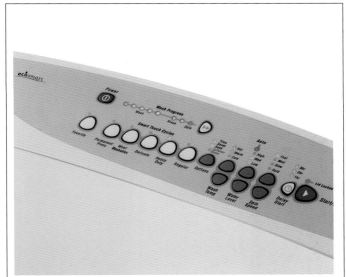

- Intelligent washers have sensors that automatically set the action and water level to suit each load.

- No more water—or energy—is used than necessary, making these machines eco-friendly.

- Most intelligent washers require nothing more than for you to select the dirt level—the machine does the rest.

- Some models have additional options, such as eco-friendly water-saver cycles.

MATTRESSES

Natural materials can make for a more comfortable—and safe—eco-friendly mattress.

Choosing the right mattress is more than a matter of personal preference. There are safety issues to consider, too. But there are ways to meet fire-retardancy rules without using harsh chemicals. Mattresses made of natural materials are both safe and environmentally sound.

Organic-wool mattresses, for instance, are free of synthetic chemicals every step of the way. The sheep are fed in organic pastures, the wool-cleaning process involves no bleach or solvents, and even the carding process is completed without chemical additives. Mattresses made of organic wool are one of the best eco-friendly options but, not surprisingly, one of the most expensive, too. Alternatively, look for mattresses

Wool Mattresses

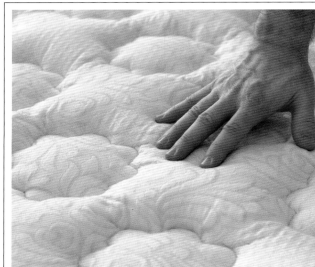

- Because wool wicks moisture away from your body, it provides a comfortable and dry sleeping surface.

- Wool is naturally resilient, so it is soothing to the body's pressure points and can even bring relief to arthritic symptoms.

- Wool mattresses are both hypoallergenic and fire-retardant.

- Some wool mattresses are best placed on slatted foundations, allowing free airflow all around them; continual airflow is how a wool mattress maintains itself.

Organic-Cotton Mattresses

- To meet federal standards, an organic-cotton mattress must have a fire retardant, such as wool, in some part of the mattress such as the innerspring or pillow top.

- Natural fibers such as cotton allow air circulation and breathability for a healthier sleeping environment.

- Organic-cotton mattresses are void of toxic chemicals that might be inhaled during sleep.

- When purchasing an innerspring mattress, make sure that the coils are chemical free, too.

that are labeled "pure wool" or "all natural." Most are chemical free in their construction.

Another organic option is cotton. Although mattresses made solely of organic cotton are available only with a doctor's prescription (a fire-retardant fiber, such as wool, must be incorporated for the mattress to meet federal safety standards), there are organic options; a mattress with an organic wool innerspring, for instance.

Natural rubber is another good mattress material; it's flexible, yet stable, providing pure comfort. And, it is absorbent and resilient, contributing to excellent heat and moisture control.

And a fiber that's long been considered green is now being used to make mattresses, too. Hemp is naturally resistant to UV light, mold, mildew and even saltwater. What's more, hemp is strong, absorbent, and insulative—even more so than cotton—which make it a natural choice for this use. What does it take to bring rubber or hemp mattresses up to safety standards? Nothing more than a protective cover that incorporates a fire-retardant fiber such as wool.

Rubber Mattresses

- Rubber is harvested by tapping the milk, or sap, of the common rubber tree. The milk of the rubber tree contains an antibacterial substance that is a natural dust-mite repellent.

- Mattresses can be 100 percent rubber or combined with innersprings.

- Natural rubber mattresses offer both flexibility and stability, as well as good air circulation, preventing the growth of mold or mildew.

- Because rubber is a natural material, it's completely biodegradable, too.

Hemp Mattresses

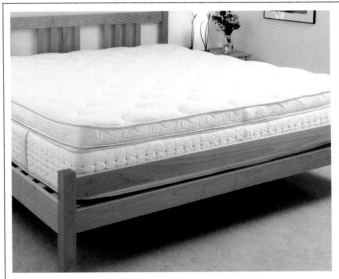

- Three times stronger than cotton, hemp fibers create a very firm mattress; the mattress itself contains hemp, and the outer covering is often made of hemp, too.

- Hemp is dense and durable, making it well suited to mattresses.

- This sustainable plant is naturally mold- and mildew-resistant.

- In order to meet fire-safety standards, hemp mattresses include a layer of wool as well as borate powder.

133

PILLOWS

There's no need to give an inch of comfort when choosing an eco-friendly pillow.

Long gone are the days when feather pillows were your only choice. Today there are all kinds of options, and many of them are green.

Pillows made of organic cotton usually come in three lofts. A light loft is a good choice for stomach sleepers, medium suits back sleepers, and full or firm is good for those who sleep on their sides. Generally, though, all cotton pillows are firmer than those filled with wool, which are characterized by more of a bouncy loft. In pillows classified as organic, the wool fill comes from organically raised sheep; the fleece is washed with nothing more than hot water and vegetable-based soaps and even carded in a chemical-free machine.

GREEN DECORATING & REMODELING

Organic Cotton

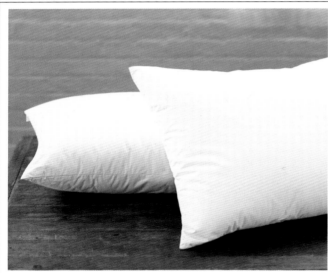

- All-cotton pillows provide a relatively flat sleeping surface.

- Cotton pillows are firmer than those made of wool and will typically compress by about one third over the life of the pillow.

- Pillows made of cotton are available in three lofts—light, medium, and full or firm.

- To get the complete hypoallergenic benefit of an organic cotton–filled pillow, cover it with an organic-cotton pillowcase.

Wool

- Pillows made of wool are soft and springy, and—like most other types—come in soft, medium, and firm support.

- Wool wicks away moisture on warm nights and insulates on cool ones.

- This natural material is hypoallergenic, resistant to dust mites, bacteria, mold, and mildew, which makes it a good choice for those people with allergies.

- Pillows made of wool are naturally flame-resistant.

The all-natural options don't stop there. Pillows made of natural rubber are available in both shredded and solid forms. Those with a shredded fill have built-in flexibility, because you can easily move the pellets around. Solid rubber pillows, on the other hand, offer more firm support while still conforming to the contours of your head.

On the opposite end of the spectrum, kapok pillows have a cotton-like softness. Harvested from the seedpods of kapok trees, this renewable resource is nature's environmentally friendly version of down.

Natural Rubber

- Pillows made of natural rubber provide firm support, breathe well, and have good ventilation.

- Natural rubber pillows are available in shredded as well as solid forms, but both easily conform to the contours of the head and neck.

- Pillows made of rubber are mold-, mildew-, and dust mite–resistant and fully washable.

- Organic-cotton pillowcases are a good green choice for natural-rubber pillows.

Kapok

- Kapok, a fiber from the seedpod of the kapok tree, has all the comfort of down but the advantage of being hypoallergenic.

- Pillows made of kapok provide good support without matting down over time.

- This type of pillow is lightweight, approximately eight times lighter than cotton.

- Because kapok should not get wet, consider using a zip-up pillow cover (in additional to your regular pillowcase) to make sure it stays clean and dry.

BLANKETS
You're sure to sleep easier with a blanket made of green materials.

Wrapping up in a blanket is comforting, but even more so when you know that it's an environmentally friendly product. Take organic cotton and wool, for instance. Proper organic certification takes time, but the results are worth the wait.

Organic cotton can take the form of a variety of textures, from a smooth jacquard weave to nubby chenille. Blankets made of organic cotton often retain their natural color—ecru or a soft mocha brown (yes, cotton does naturally grow in this color)—but can be found in limited colors, too. The one thing they all have in common, however, is their inherent softness. Likewise, blankets made of organic wool are soft and soothing. And because wool is such a great insulator, it's

Organic Cotton

- Blankets made of organic cotton are available in various types and textures, including woven jacquard and chenille.

- Cotton blankets are soft and cozy by nature.

- In their most natural state, organic-cotton blankets are either ecru or mocha in color, the latter made from a special cotton that has a warm mocha hue.

- This blanket is a good choice for people who have chemical sensitivities.

Organic Wool

- Blankets made of organic wool are naturally soft, free of mothproofing and other toxic chemicals.

- Because wool is warm in winter and cool in summer, these blankets can be used year-round.

- Organic wool is naturally nonallergenic and resistant to dust mites, mold, mildew, and odors.

- Although wool blankets can typically be hand washed or machine washed on a delicate cycle, they should never be put in the dryer.

comfortable in all temperatures, every month of the year.

If it's luxury you want, look no further than silk. Blankets made of this fiber have a delicate look, but that belies the natural durability of the material. Natural silk is superior in strength to any other plant or animal fiber. If you like the look of silk, but not the cost, consider a less-expensive alternative—a blanket made of bamboo. Not only do bamboo blankets have a similar silky appearance, but they're also quite warm relative to their actual weight.

········· GREEN ● LIGHT ·········

It's naturally a good idea to recycle your blankets in some way, but you can purchase blankets made of recycled fabrics, too. You'll find them made out of a variety of items, including repurposed sweaters and jersey T-shirts. The ultimate recycled blanket, however, is one made of all-natural materials.

Silk

- Blankets made of silk are lightweight and luxurious, although they can be expensive.

- Silk is naturally hypoallergenic, resistant to dust mites (which can cause allergies and asthma), moisture, and mildew.

- Silk fibers contain amino acids, which are good for both the hair and the skin, and even thought by some to relieve the aches and pains of arthritis.

- A single silk blanket is recommended for summer, two for winter.

Bamboo

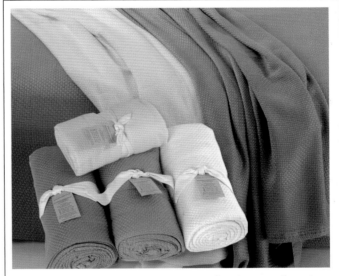

- In woven forms, such as blankets, bamboo is soft, smooth, and luxurious—not unlike silk.

- Although bamboo blankets are lightweight, they're quite warm.

- Bamboo is naturally resistant to germ and bacteria growth, an advantage for those who suffer from allergies.

- Blankets made of bamboo provide superior ventilation and wicking properties, making them comfortable any time of the year.

ALL THE EXTRAS

Mattress pads and toppers, barrier cloths—even futons—can enhance a good night's sleep.

Even the best mattress can be made even better with just a small addition or two. A mattress pad, for instance, can provide more than a protective surface for the mattress itself. The right one can add an extra layer of comfort, not to mention health benefits. A hypoallergenic pad, for instance, can be a real plus for an allergy sufferer. Similarly, an eco-friendly mattress topper in wool or natural rubber can offer the same health benefits but, because it's thicker, ups the comfort quotient, too. Those made of rubber are firm while still conforming easily to your body. Wool, on the other hand, is a better choice for those who prefer lofty, sink-into comfort. And, to take environmental awareness one step further, you

Mattress Pads

- A mattress pad can extend the life of any mattress.

- An organic-cotton mattress pad—organic-cotton batting wrapped in organic cotton fabric—provides a thinner pad, making it easier to slip sheets over the mattress and pad.

- Wool mattress pads are hypoallergenic and soft while providing a barrier against dust mites.

- Mattress pads made of natural rubber provide cushy comfort while relieving aches and pains from body pressure points.

Mattress Toppers

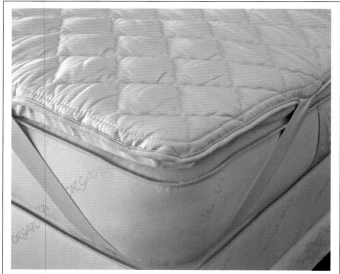

- A mattress topper is typically two inches thick or more.

- Organic-wool toppers provide extra loft to a mattress, good for people who like to sleep on a soft bed.

- Toppers made of natural rubber are thicker than rubber mattress pads, providing an extra layer of comfort, too.

- Organic cotton is often used as the shell for wool and rubber toppers but not for the fill, because it would flatten too much over time.

can even protect your mattress and box spring with barrier cloths made of organic cotton.

Likewise, it's easier than ever to find futons that are completely green. These alternatives to conventional mattresses have come a long way since the days when they mainly found homes in dorm rooms and first apartments. Today's versions—constructed of materials such as wool, hemp, cotton, and natural rubber—are just as versatile as ever, if not more so. But they're better made than the originals, making them more durable, too.

Organic Cotton Barrier Cloths

- A barrier cloth fits over a mattress, box springs, or even pillow in much the same way as a pillow case but with a zipper enclosure.

- An organic-cotton barrier cloth with a high thread count will protect a mattress from dust mites, mold, and dander.

- Because organic cotton is hypoallergenic, it makes for easier sleeping, too.

- Barrier cloths made of organic cotton are machine washable.

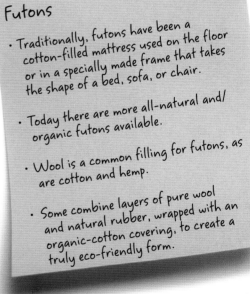

Futons
- Traditionally, futons have been a cotton-filled mattress used on the floor or in a specially made frame that takes the shape of a bed, sofa, or chair.

- Today there are more all-natural and/ organic futons available.

- Wool is a common filling for futons, as are cotton and hemp.

- Some combine layers of pure wool and natural rubber, wrapped with an organic-cotton covering, to create a truly eco-friendly form.

BATH LINENS

By adding natural elements to the bath, you'll naturally help the environment, too.

It's easier than you might think to be more eco-friendly in the bathroom. Say, for instance, you've had all-cotton towels for years. Why not trade out those old towels for thick, thirsty ones made of organic cotton or bamboo? Organic-cotton towels are more readily available all the time, either in conventional loop styles or waffle weaves. There's no need to think that you're limited in terms of color, either. Low eco-impact dyes are being used more every day, which ultimately will allow you to color coordinate your room any way you like. And then there's bamboo. The same fiber that's used to create silky-soft sheets can be transformed into absorbent towels, also in a wide variety of hues.

Cotton Towels

- Bath towels made of organic cotton are soft and become even more so with each washing.

- Chlorine- and softener-free finishing preserves the inherent softness of organic-cotton towels.

- This type of towel comes in several weights; the heavier the towel, the more absorbent it is.

- Organic-cotton towels are most often off-white, cotton's natural hue, but can also be colored with low eco-impact dyes.

Bamboo Towels

- Bath towels made of bamboo are naturally antibacterial and luxuriously soft.

- This type of towel is very lightweight, yet highly absorbent and quick drying, too.

- Bamboo towels should be machine washed on delicate and tumble dried low. Neither bleach nor fabric softeners should be used.

- Towels made of all bamboo are available in limited colors, while those that combine bamboo and cotton have a broader range.

Likewise, the proliferation of vinyl shower curtains is rapidly giving way to those made of cotton, linen, and hemp. All are good choices for the bath, as they naturally resist mold and mildew. Some reflect the fibers' natural colors, but more are showing up in colors and patterns. Last but not least, rugs are essential to any bathroom, providing warmth—and safety—from the first moment you step out of the shower or tub. Natural cotton, bamboo, and hemp are not only eco-friendly, but they're naturally more absorbent than synthetics, too.

ZOOM

Today, there are surprising new fibers being used in towels. Some are made from a combination of 70 percent wood fiber (from managed forests) and 30 percent cotton, creating towels that are soft and absorbent. Even silk is being used to produce towels that are lightweight, absorbent, and very soft to the touch.

Shower Curtains

- Shower curtains made of organic-cotton canvas naturally repel water.

- Organic-cotton shower curtains are also available in light-weight fabrics, some with patterns.

- Because the flax used for linen is grown without harmful pesticides, linen shower curtains are more resistant to mold and mildew.

- Shower curtains made of hemp, known for its strength and durability, are naturally antifungal and antibacterial.

Rugs

- Organic-cotton rugs are a good choice in the bathroom, as they provide warmth and softness underfoot.

- Plush bamboo rugs come in a variety of colors, absorb water quickly, and are antibacterial, too.

- Hemp rugs, available in limited colors, absorb up to 150 percent of their weight in water.

- Another green option for the bathroom is to use a recycled rug, or one made of recycled materials.

SINKS

If a sink is durable or recyclable, it gets a "green" light, too.

Many sinks fall into one of two eco-friendly categories or even both: They're durable, meaning they won't have to be replaced for years to come, or they're made of recyclable materials.

Metal sinks remain the hands-down most popular option—those made of stainless steel, brass, copper, or bronze as well as steel that's been thin coated with porcelain. Likewise, heavy-duty cast iron falls into this category, and it's easily the most durable of the bunch. If it's durability you're looking for, though, metal isn't your only option; be sure to consider stone or concrete, too. Due to their porous nature, sinks made of stone or concrete typically require a seal of some

Metal

Stone

- Metal sink options go far beyond conventional stainless steel to include brass, copper, and bronze.

- These types of metals are recyclable and easy to clean, but are vulnerable to scratches, so abrasive cleaners are not recommended.

- Cast-iron sinks are coated with an enamel finish and are available in assorted styles, from traditional undermounts to contemporary vessels.

- If the enamel surface of a cast-iron sink chips or scratches.

- Sinks made of stone come in materials such as granite, soapstone, travertine, and marble.

- Due to the porous nature of stone, sinks should be sealed to protect them against staining and water absorption.

- Stone sinks can be sealed with wax or a commercial stone-sealing product, preferably one that is considered green.

- An increasingly popular alternative to stone is concrete, and it can be colored, too.

kind, but that can be accomplished with a coat of wax.

Glass sinks, meanwhile, have become a hot commodity, particularly in bathrooms and powder rooms. Solid-glass basins are available in virtually any color, and they can be made of mosaics, too. Plus, the glass can be recycled again. Among the latest trends are sinks made of bamboo. Crafted of cross-laminated strips of the bamboo stalk and protected with a nontoxic polyurethane resin, bamboo sinks take a minimal toll on the environment. Their increasing popularity means they're becoming available in more styles, too.

Glass

- Sinks made of glass are durable enough to withstand everyday wear.

- Glass sinks are typically able to tolerate temperature changes of up to 70 degrees without breakage, although you should avoid pouring scalding hot water into them.

- Be aware that heavy objects will shatter a glass sink, just as they would porcelain.

- One of the best attributes of glass is that it's completely recyclable.

Bamboo

- Sinks made of sustainable bamboo are constructed of cross-laminated strips of the bamboo stalk.

- To keep this type of sink watertight, it has a protective layer of nontoxic polyurethane resin.

- Numerous bamboo sinks are available in the material's natural honey color, but you'll also find other shades—even bright hues—thanks to the addition of water-based dyes.

- Freestanding bamboo sinks are available as well as contemporary vessels.

BATHTUBS

Careful tub choices can go a long way in the effort to keep a bathroom green.

Considering the amount of water it uses alone, a bathtub is by no means the most eco-friendly item you'll find. But if a bathtub is on your wish list, there are some choices—in terms of materials—that are better than others.

Bathtubs made of porcelain on steel remain one of the most popular choices, not only because they're durable but also because that they come in a wide variety of styles and colors. They're less expensive and more lightweight than bathtubs made of cast iron, though the latter has its advantages, too. Cast iron, for instance, is less susceptible to dents and dings, and its sheer density keeps bathwater hot longer.

Having gained popularity as a countertop material, con-

Porcelain on Steel

Cast Iron

- Among the most common types of bathtubs, this one is characterized by a steel shell that's been coated with heat-fused porcelain enamel.

- This type of bathtub is less expensive than cast iron and more lightweight, too.

- Porcelain-on-steel tubs are resistant to acid, corrosion, and abrasion, making their life spans longer. However, if the surface chips, it may rust.

- Less-expensive porcelain-on-steel bathtubs can be noisy.

- Enamel-coated cast iron is one of the most durable materials used to make bathtubs; the thickness of the cast iron makes it resistant to scratches and dents.

- Even if the bathtub should get scratched, it's more cost-effective to refinish it than to replace it.

- The thick metal helps keep water hot longer, too.

- Because cast-iron bathtubs can weigh between 200 and 300 pounds, extra floor support may be needed.

crete is now also being used to make bathtubs. It's as hard yet lighter than many types of stone and can be customized with color as well as texture. That said, concrete bathtubs typically require extra floor support and most often must be poured in place. But bathtub options don't stop there. You'll also find stylish tubs made of copper, teak (from managed forests, of course), and even a variety of recycled materials, including one that combines concrete and glass.

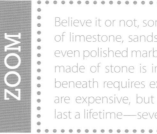
Concrete

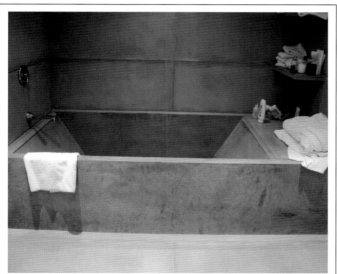

- Concrete can be formed into any shape, allowing you to have a completely custom bathtub.

- This material can be enhanced with practically any color or texture.

- Concrete is warm to the touch and harder than most kinds of stone.

- A bathtub made of concrete requires a sealer, and, due to the tub's weight, the floor typically needs extra support.

More Great Bathtubs

- Some bathtubs are now being made of a material called IceStone®, which consists of recycled glass and concrete.

- A 100 percent recyclable material called Durat is being used to create contemporary bathtubs in a wide variety of colors.

- Teak from sustainable, renewable forests can be used to create tubs for indoors or out. Likewise, copper bathtubs are handsome, and the material itself it a great conductor of heat.

147

SHOWERHEADS

Low-flow showerheads let you start every day in an eco-friendly way.

With all the talk about water conservation, you may not realize how easy it is to do your share. And that's especially true in the shower. If your house is more than fifteen years old, it's probably fitted with showerheads that use 5 to 8 gallons of water per minute—more than the now federally mandated 2.5 gallons per minute or less. Happily, though, it's easy to retrofit any shower with the low-flow variety.

Both inexpensive and easy to install, low-flow showerheads are available in both aerating and nonaerating varieties. One delivers more of a mist and the other a solid stream of water, but both are equally efficient. Both, too, can reduce your home water consumption as much as 50 percent, therefore

Aerating Low-Flow Showerheads

- This type of showerhead mixes air into the water stream, creating a steady pressure.

- Because the water is aerated into a strong mist, it can provide the added benefit of improving circulation.

- The downside of air being mixed in is that the water temperature can have a tendency to cool down a little as it reaches the floor.

- Like any other showerhead, aerating low-flow models are available with a variety of settings and sprays.

Non-Aerating Low-Flow Showerheads

- In this type of low-flow showerhead, air is not mixed into the stream, creating a strong flow of water.

- The water flow pulses in nonaerating showerheads, resulting in a massage-like effect.

- Most nonaerating showerheads are adjustable, allowing you to increase or decrease the force of the spray.

- The temperature of the water is consistent. It's the same from the moment it comes out of the showerhead until it hits the floor.

reducing your energy costs by about the same amount. Some even have options that help you save more, such as a "pause" button that allows you to completely stop the water flow while you apply soap or shampoo.

You'll also find showerheads that, in addition to being low flow, remove chlorine, bacteria, and other impurities, and some filters that go a step further to add back traces of more healthy minerals. For just a few dollars and no more than a few minutes of your time, what could be simpler?

MAKE IT EASY

Not sure if your shower has a low-flow head? Put it to the test by seeing how long it takes to fill a one-gallon bucket. If it fills up in ten seconds, the flow rate is about 6 gallons per minute. If your shower's fitted with a low-flow head, it should take twenty-five seconds or more.

PLUMBING PRODUCTS

Shower Filter

- Some shower filters not only makes the water cleaner but healthier, too.

- This type of filter can remove bacteria, heavy metals, chlorine, sediment, and other impurities from the water.

- It also re-ionizes dissolved oxygen for an antioxidant effect, and puts back in healthy trace amounts of silica, potassium, and magnesium.

- A filter like this can be attached to any standard shower, with any type of showerhead.

Rainfall Showerhead

- Rainfall showerheads are also available in low-flow models, some with health-oriented filters.

- Some use a filtering system that reduces up to 99 percent of the chlorine in treated water.

- These showerheads can also reduce amounts of hydrogen sulfide, lead, iron, mercury, calcium carbonate, and magnesium, as well as bacteria and algae.

- The filters on these types of showerheads usually need to be replaced every six to nine months.

FAUCETS
You can keep money from going down the drain by using an efficient faucet.

Like showerheads, faucets come in low-flow versions that are easy to install. For a kitchen faucet, you may want a 2.5-gallons-per-minute flow to make sure you can efficiently wash and rinse dishes. In the bathroom, however, 1.5 to 2 gallons per minute is perfectly adequate for hygiene needs, nowhere near the 5-gallons-per-minute output of some lavatory faucets.

Low-flow faucets have built-in aerators that mix air into the water as it leaves the spout, reducing both the water flow and the amount that it splashes. If you're buying a new faucet, look for one that doesn't have any lead solder—a relatively new exposure to lead that's come to light.

If switching out your old faucet for a low-flow model simply

Low-Flow Faucets

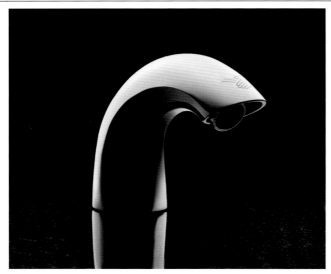

- Any faucet with an output of 2.5 gallons or less is considered low flow.

- Green Seal® has a certification standard of 2 gallons per minute for lavatory faucets and 2.5 gallons per minute for kitchen faucets.

- In low-flow faucets, built-in aerators mix air into the water as it leaves the faucet, reducing both the flow and the amount of splash.

- Replacing an entire faucet is more costly than fitting an old one with an aerator.

Faucet Aerators

- Aerators can be retrofitted onto almost any faucet, reducing the water flow to approximately 3 gallons per minute.

- The screened metal disks screw onto the head of the faucet, increasing pressure and mixing air with the water.

- Aerators for kitchen faucets are available with a variety of spray patterns as well as flow-control options.

- Because there can be a buildup of grit and scale, periodic cleaning is required.

isn't possible, consider retrofitting the one you have with an aerator. Faucet aerators are circular screened disks, typically made of metal, that easily screw onto the head of a faucet to reduce water flow. Though not quite as efficient as low-flow faucets, they will reduce the output to around 3 gallons per minute. Like low-flow faucets, however, aerators reduce water flow and increase the pressure, incorporating air as the water comes from the tap. At less than five dollars, an aera-

tor is a bargain that homeowners—as well as renters—can't afford to pass up. And as long as you're making your faucet more efficient, why not purify the water, too? Water filters in a variety of styles can tap right into the faucet.

Last but not least, be sure to conserve every drop of water by keeping a watchful eye out for leaks. More often than not, you can fix them yourself—and save money in the process.

Faucet-Mount Water Purifiers

- Water filters improve the taste of tap water by removing impurities, handling between 60 to 100 gallons before needing to be changed.

- A faucet mount is a good choice if you regularly use filtered water for ice cubes or to make coffee.

- Some have a bypass feature that allows you to switch back and forth between filtered and unfiltered water.

- Because this type of filter is attached to a faucet, leakage is possible between the two elements.

Stop a Leaky Faucet

- Water loss caused by dripping faucets can waste from several gallons to several hundred gallons.

- Make it a regular habit to check for leaks at the faucet head, the base, and all connections.

- Leaks can typically be repaired by simply replacing washers and/or tightening the faucet stem.

- A wide variety of repair kits can be found in hardware and home improvement stores.

KEEP IT CLEAN

Cleaning products can be completely nontoxic and still get the job done beautifully.

If you've gone to all the trouble of buying environmentally friendly home furnishings, why negate your good works by cleaning with something that isn't green? For all-purpose products, you'll want something that's nontoxic and biodegradable, a cleaner that works as well on stubborn counter stains as it does on your best crystal.

The right laundry detergent can make a big difference, too, not only on the environment but also your personal well-being. After wash day, any petrochemical residue that's left on your clothes will come directly in contact with your skin. And that, in turn, can cause rashes, allergies, and many other health problems for the entire family. Consider the same

All-Purpose Cleaners

- The most nontoxic cleaners are formulated to be phosphate free, biodegradable, and nonflammable, with no harmful dyes, fragrances, or hazardous ingredients.

- Look for cleaners that are Green Seal certified.

- All-purpose varieties will clean everything from windows to countertops, stainless steel to TV screens.

- If the cleaning solution needs to be mixed with water, opt for one that works with cold water in order to save valuable energy.

Laundry Detergents

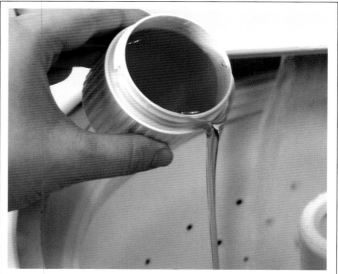

- The best eco-friendly detergents are made without nonrenewable, petroleum-based chemicals and are biodegradable, without toxic dyes or fragrances.

- If you prefer soap instead of detergent, look for an all-natural liquid made without artificial dyes or fragrances.

- You'll find all-purpose detergents and special formulas for delicates, baby clothes, and people with chemical sensitivities.

- Soap flakes are also available, often a good choice for those with sensitive skin.

concept when it comes to the dishwashing detergent you use. Do you really want to eat from a plate that's been coated with a petroleum-based "cleaner"? Even specialty cleaners, like those for the shower, should be non-toxic and biodegradable. Those that are hydrogen peroxide–based will get the job done without unpleasant fumes or harmful residues.

Once you've replaced your old cleaning products with those that are green, dispose of the old ones in a responsible way. Check their labels for instructions and follow them to the letter.

ZOOM

In addition to all of the eco-friendly cleaning products available today, there are plenty as close as your own pantry, too. Take a little time to research some homemade solutions. You may be surprised at what you can do with nothing more than a little white vinegar and baking soda.

Dishwashing Detergents

- Liquid dish detergents that are eco-friendly are vegetable based instead of petroleum based.

- Look for key words on the detergent's label such as nontoxic, biodegradable, unscented, dye free, and phosphate free.

- For dishwashers, use powders or liquids that have neither chlorine nor phosphates.

- You'll find that some varieties incorporate a natural oxygen bleach to get rid of stains and/or citrus extracts to fight odors.

Natural Shower Cleaners

- To remove soap scum and stains caused by mold and mildew in the shower, use a nontoxic cleaner that is biodegradable.

- Those that are hydrogen peroxide based are more eco-friendly than those that contain chlorine bleach.

- Unlike many conventional shower cleaners, those with hydrogen peroxide don't produce unpleasant fumes or harmful residues.

- Some cleaners are scented, but those with natural fragrances are the most green.

BEDS

Creating a safe and healthy haven is imperative for a baby's nursery.

When shopping for baby's crib or bassinet, safety should be the top priority. But an infant's sleeping spot needs to be environmentally sound, too.

Cribs, for instance, have traditionally been made of wood—or at least made to look like it. To ensure your child's safety from a green point of view, make sure that a crib is made of solid hardwood, preferably taken from well-managed forests. But your eco-friendly perspective shouldn't stop there, either. Every detail on a baby's sleeping spot, down to the last drop of glue, needs to be nontoxic in order to create an entirely safe surround. As an alternative to all-wood cribs, some of today's most innovative designs incorporate upholstered

Wooden Cribs

- Birch and solid maple are often used to make cribs, as are a variety of hardwoods, the best of which come from sustainable forests.

- Medium-density fiberboard (MDF) should be avoided, unless it's made of recovered wood fibers.

- All materials used to construct a crib—including paints, stains, and glues—should be nontoxic.

- For safety purposes, many of today's cribs feature fixed side rails and/or lower centers of gravity.

Upholstered Cribs

- Upholstered headboards and footboards soften a crib's design, adding to the safety factor, too; there's less likelihood baby will bump his or her head.

- Only natural fabrics should be used, such as cotton or wool, hemp, and linen.

- All materials—right down to the glue—should be nontoxic.

- Some models incorporate built-in storage beneath the bed or can be converted to toddler beds.

headboards and footboards. But, like their wooden counterparts, these baby beds should be entirely green, using natural fabrics such as organic cotton or durable hemp.

Even more portable beds, such as bassinets and Moses baskets, should meet green standards, as should any mattresses and bumper pads used with them. Likewise, supportive platforms, most often made of wood, must be safe both structurally and environmentally.

Getting your baby off to the right start, in a healthy environment, is one of the best things you can do for him or her.

Moses Baskets

- The all-natural Moses basket has long been a favorite sleeping spot for newborns.

- The accompanying bed linens should be as eco-friendly as the basket itself; fabrics such as organic cotton are a good green choice.

- In addition to its eco-friendly attributes, a Moses basket is both lightweight and portable.

- The basket can be used alone or set on top of a rocker made especially for it.

Bassinets

- Bassinets are available in more styles than ever and an increasing number meet green standards.

- Typically used for infants up to twenty pounds, bassinets can be made of hardwoods, organic fabrics, or woven from natural materials.

- Bassinets are typically designed to be set on a platform, whether it's stationary or a rocker style.

- Some can be converted to serve other purposes, such as a changing table, once the baby has outgrown it for sleeping.

NURSERY

BED LINENS
With the right bedding choices, your baby will sleep better and so will you.

During the first year of their lives, babies spend more than half their time sleeping—and much of that time is in their cribs. So why wouldn't you choose eco-friendly bed linens?

Crib sheets made of organic cotton are readily available in their natural, undyed state as well as those in pastel colors and whimsical patterns. Not all cotton sheets are standard percale, either. Other options include flannel, sateen, and knit jersey—just as soft as your favorite T-shirt. And if nothing's too good for your little prince or princess, silk sheets are also available.

Likewise, blankets come in organic fabrics, ranging from soft brushed cotton to felted wool. Because they're just as soft as

Crib Sheets

- Some of the most eco-friendly sheets are those made of 100 percent organic cotton.

- Cotton sheets can be found in standard percale as well as cozy flannel, silky sateen, and woven interlock (jersey).

- Natural, undyed cotton sheets are a good choice for a baby's delicate skin, although they also come in baby-safe patterns and colors.

- For a touch of pure luxury, consider crib sheets made of silk.

Blankets

- Organic-cotton blankets are lightweight and good insulators, while wool has similar insulative properties and is a natural fire retardant.

- Silk-filled blankets typically have either silk or cotton coverings.

- Bamboo fibers are used to create silk-like blankets, while recycled blankets are made from old sweaters and even recycled bottles.

- Quilts made of all cotton work well in the crib or as playmats, while wool- and silk-filled comforters are available in crib sizes, too.

baby's skin, blankets made of delicate silk or silklike bamboo are good choices and, perhaps surprisingly, blankets made from recycled soda pop bottles can be equally gentle to the touch. And to tuck your little one in safe and sound, line the crib with an all-natural bumper pad.

Finally, the right mattress can make a world of difference. Both innerspring and noninnerspring styles come in organic cotton and/or wool, and all-natural rubber also provides a supportive sleeping surface. On the other hand, if you're looking for something really soft, consider a crib-size cotton futon.

A mattress pad is a must in any crib in order to keep it clean and dry. One pad is good, but layering two is even better. Placed directly under the crib sheet, this type of pad—which can be found in organic fabrics—keeps any wetness from reaching the mattress itself.

Bumper Pads

- Organic cotton and organic wool are often used for bumper pads, in both the filling as well as the outer shell.

- Some bumper pads require covers while others do not, but those with covers are easier to keep clean.

- Likewise, some bumper pads are machine washable and others are not.

- Bumper pad covers, as well as any embellishments such as embroidery and ties, should be as natural as the linens themselves.

Mattresses

- Innerspring mattresses, the most conventional type, come in organic cotton, organic wool, and some that combine the two fibers.

- Noninnerspring mattresses are preferred by people concerned with the electromagnetic fields—caused by the metal springs.

- Natural rubber mattresses are metal free, with a supportive core of rubber that's often wrapped with cotton or wool.

- As an alternative to a standard mattress, you'll find crib-size futons made of organic cotton.

NURSERY

SEATING AND STORAGE

Furniture in the nursery can be just as versatile as it is eco-friendly.

Not surprisingly, babies are more vulnerable to environmental pollutants than adults. So give your newborn every advantage by creating a safe, healthy haven.

A place for mother and child to sit is requisite for any nursery. And because so much time is spent sitting in this room, it's important that the chair be not only comfortable but nontoxic, too. One option is the classic wood rocking chair. The best upholstered chairs are those made of sustainable wood frames and covered in natural fabrics like cotton, linen, or hemp. But look deeper to make sure that all filling, coils, and fasteners are nontoxic, too.

In the search for the perfect storage pieces, look for armoires

Upholstered Seating

- An upholstered chair is a comfortable choice for a nursery, especially one that's set on rockers.

- Eco-friendly options include those with sustainable wood frames that are covered in natural fabrics, such as cotton, linen, and hemp.

- Soft upholstery is safe, too, once a baby starts to crawl.

- Upholstered chairs are often more expensive than all-wood types, but can be moved to another bedroom or even the family room once they're no longer needed in the nursery.

Wooden Rocker

- A wooden rocker has long been the traditional seating piece of choice for the nursery.

- Rockers made of sustainable woods from well-managed forests are the most desirable.

- Be sure that all finishes and glues are nontoxic, too.

- Handmade rockers are most often the most eco-friendly; they may cost a bit more but can be handed down for generations to come.

that are not only green but also versatile enough to work well for years to come. The right one can, for example, hold baby's wardrobe now and home electronics in the family room later. Chests—solid wood pieces in particular—have the same ability to work in multiple rooms once they've served their original purpose in the nursery. But other options for the baby's room also include storage made of natural materials such as wicker, rattan, and bamboo. Keep your eye out for furniture that is green and innovative, too, such as dressers that use canvas to fashion soft-sided drawers.

Armoires

Chests

- An armoire is a good choice for a nursery because it can grow up with your child and be useful for years to come.

- One-piece armoires are most common, but you'll find them in stackable designs, too.

- All-wood types—with no veneers, plywood, or particleboard—are good choices, but those made of sustainable woods are even better.

- Like any eco-friendly piece of furniture, finishes and finishing details should be nontoxic, too.

- Solid wood chests and dressers are good options for a nursery, as are those made of bamboo.

- Avoid furnishings made with plywood, particleboard, and medium-density fiberboard (MDF) because they often contain formaldehyde in their glues.

- Some chests are made with hardwood or bamboo frames, then fitted with drawers made of cotton canvas.

- Soft-sided storage pieces like these are particularly good when a baby starts to crawl.

WALL AND WINDOW COVERINGS

A healthy environment for any nursery starts with the shell of the room.

From top to bottom, nurseries need to be nontoxic. And, considering their expansive surfaces, that starts with the walls and windows.

Painted walls are an inexpensive and versatile design solution, but, at the same time, paints can be highly toxic. Low-VOC (Volatile Organic Compounds) varieties are good but those with no VOCs are even better. Some companies have come out with paints formulated specifically for children's rooms. Likewise, milk paints are available in powder form,

To find out which companies carry nontoxic paints that match your scheme, go to www.colorcharts.org.

Paint

- Paints used in a nursery should have low or no VOCs.

- Some earth-conscious paint companies have come out with nontoxic coverings that have been formulated especially for the nursery.

- Low- and no-VOC paints, as well as specialty coverings, are available in a variety of colors.

- Some of these paints can be applied to a wide variety of surfaces, including concrete and brick.

Milk Paint

- Milk paint, usually found in powder form, contains milk protein, lime, clay, and earth pigments such as ochre, umber, iron oxide, and lampblack.

- This product replicates the paint once made with skim milk or buttermilk and crushed limestone.

- The dry powder can be hydrated to the thickness of a wash or a full-cover coat.

- Basic colors are limited but can be mixed to form other hues.

containing nothing more than milk protein, lime, clay, and earth pigments for color. The bottom line, though, is that you should look for paints that are as natural as possible.

In terms of window treatments, cotton curtains are a perennially popular choice. At the least, look for all-cotton curtains with no chemical finish on the fabric itself. At best, opt for those made of organic cotton. While the latter may not offer as many decorative options, you can take matters into your own hands by purchasing organic cotton yardage and sew-

ing your own one-of-a-kind design. You might choose to utilize the fabric in its natural state or add natural dyes to give it some color. You could even use organic cotton ribbon in lieu of conventional tie-backs.

But one of the simplest window solutions is an all-natural shade. Made of natural fibers such as bamboo, reeds, and exotic grasses, these shades are as handsome in their own right as they are coupled with curtains.

Organic-Cotton Curtains

- Cotton curtains are readily available for nurseries, but those made of organic cotton are the best choice.

- Organic cotton is more earth-friendly than conventional cotton, plus it's less toxic and, as a result, more child friendly, too.

- If you can't find the style of curtains you're looking for, purchase organic-cotton yardage and sew them yourself.

- Using natural dyes, yardage can be colored to coordinate with your nursery scheme.

Natural-Fiber Shades

- Window shades made of renewable fibers such as bamboo and grass are non-toxic.

- The neutral hues of these window coverings make them compatible with any decor.

- To keep a baby's room dark during naptime, look for shades that are backed with blackout material.

- Natural-fiber shades can be used alone or coupled with curtains—those made of organic cotton, for instance, are a good green choice.

GENERAL LIGHTING

It has never been easier to illuminate your home in an energy-efficient way.

General, or ambient, lighting is—on the most basic level—what allows you to walk through a room with ease. No tripping over toys. No stubbing your toes. One of the most common types of lights in this category is the simple ceiling fixture. Typically placed in the center of the ceiling, this type of lighting casts an overall soft glow throughout a room.

And, if it's an energy-efficient fluorescent, so much the better. Track lights, too, are a good general lighting choice; they allow you to adjust their moveable fixtures to best suit your room. While the first track lights were purely contemporary, today's versions cover the style gamut.

Just as advancements are being made to conserve the

Energy Efficient

- Fluorescent fixtures of any kind are some of the most energy efficient that you will find.

- There's a safety factor involved, too, because fluorescents operate in a cooler manner than their incandescent counterparts.

- Fixtures like this brushed aluminum example (above) diffuse and softly reflect light back into the room.

- Fitted with circular compact fluorescent bulbs (CFLs), as opposed to conventional fluorescents, fixtures like this one can produce more light with less energy.

Low Voltage

- By definition, low-voltage lighting operates at 30 volts or less.

- Low-voltage lights typically produce more than twice as much light as incandescents; a 50-watt low-voltage lamp, for example, generates as much light as a 125-watt incandescent.

- To make a home's standard 120-volt current suitable for low-voltage lighting, transformers are built right into the fixtures, bringing the current down to 12 volts.

- Low-voltage track lighting is available in a variety of styles.

amount of energy any light uses, more designs—particularly in pendant lamps—are taking advantage of recycled materials, too. Everything from tin to disposable wine glasses are being used to create stunning fixtures. These innovative lighting solutions even include pendants made of 100 percent wool, needing nothing more than eco-friendly compact fluorescent bulbs. You'll find pendant lights with shades that have open tops and/or bottoms, and others that are completely enclosed. Which fixture best suits you depends on how much, or how little, light you want to shed.

Recycled

- Coupled with energy-efficient bulbs, fixtures made of recycled materials make a completely green light source.

- There's no limit to the types of reclaimed items that are being transformed into lamps.

- Pendant lights, like this one made of scrap tin, lead the way in terms of recycled styles.

- The flexibility of pendant lights makes them attractive, too, because they can be used in a variety of rooms.

Innovative

- Some of today's most innovative lighting is being created with eco-friendly natural materials.

- This pendant lamp is made from two all-wool shells; the darker color directs the light downward, while the lighter one softly diffuses it.

- Designed to be used alone or in multiples, this fixture accommodates a compact fluorescent light bulb.

- Easily disassembled, this fixture can ultimately be returned to the manufacturer for recycling.

LIGHTING

TASK LIGHTING

Look for task lights that are as easy on the environment as they are on your eyes.

As its name implies, task lighting focuses light where you need it most—on the book that you're reading, the salad you're making, even the lipstick you're applying. Pendant, table, and floor lamps are often used to shed task lighting. And some of today's green options have the flexibility to work in more than one way. That kind of flexibility enhances the eco-friendly factor, as the fixture can move from room to room, or even from home to home, with no replacement needed! There are those lamps, too, that simulate solar light, known to be easier on the eyes. These fixtures typically operate on nothing more than a 27-watt compact fluorescent bulb (CFL), making them energy savers.

Energy Efficient

- The packaging of this light becomes part of the shade, making it the epitome of efficiency.

- An energy-efficient bulb is included with the lamp, so it can be assembled—and working—in a matter of minutes.

- The lamp's design allows it to be used as either a table lamp or a pendant.

- Every aspect of this light is eco-friendly; the shade is recyclable and even the instructions are printed on recycled paper, using environmentally friendly inks, of course.

Solar Substitute

- Lamps like this one simulate Mother Nature's sunshine to produce glare-free light.

- One of the benefits of this type of light is that it reduces eyestrain.

- Both the table lamp and floor lamp styles operate on a 27-watt CFL that produces the same amount of light as a 100-watt incandescent.

- The adjustable gooseneck design makes it good for close-up tasks, such as reading and needlework.

That's not to say that conventional table lamps are out of the picture. On the contrary, fitting one with a CFL immediately makes it more green. Even better, though, is if the lamp is made of recycled materials. Bases of table lamps are as innovative as pendant fixtures, but some recycled options aren't obvious. Bases made of recycled brass, for instance, may not appear to be anything but brand-new. Conversely, some other task lights are so innovative that they double as artwork. That kind of efficiency plays right into the green scheme of things.

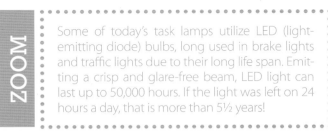
Recycled

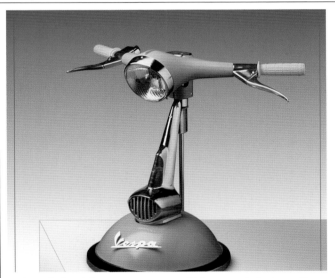

- Recycled task lamps come in styles ranging from contemporary to traditional.

- Some of the most innovative examples incorporate elements from bikes and motor scooters.

- This example features the original handlebars of a Vespa scooter.

- Look around the house for elements that can be transformed into lamp bases; a professional can transform almost anything into a lamp.

Innovative

- When looking for task lamps, don't forget about the not-so-obvious ones, such as nightlights to lead you from the bedroom to the bath in the middle of the night.

- The artistic solution makes this nightlight appropriate for any room, for all ages.

- This one features a leaf that's been preserved in iridescent minerals.

- The light shines softly from around the small fixture and through the leaf's veining, too.

LIGHTING

169

ACCENT LIGHTING

The right accent light can showcase a room's best features, and do so in a green way.

A well-lit room should have a balanced mix of general (ambient), task, and accent lighting. Because accent lighting focuses on certain pieces—such as paintings and sculptures—it needs to be brighter than the room's general lighting, meaning that it traditionally takes more energy, too. But, with the advent of more efficient bulbs, that has changed.

Today, you can get the same strong beam of light in a much more energy-efficient way.

Accent lighting can come from any number of sources, depending on the mood you're trying to create. Track lights, for instance, can be pinpointed to focus on a work of art, or the piece might be flanked by a pair of sconces, framing it in an

Energy Efficient

- Wall-mounted sconces, which can provide general or accent lighting, conserve precious floor space.

- The style of the sconce as well as the material dictates how much, or how little, light it gives off.

- The one above offers limited, directional lighting, so it falls into the accent category—perfect for shedding light on artwork, for instance.

- To keep it energy efficient, this sconce is made to accommodate (CFLs).

Sustainable

- With a long and narrow shade created from cork, this accent lamp is sustainable in nature and has a decorative aspect, too.

- The two bulbs within shine through the paper-thin cork shade, resulting in a softly filtered light.

- Even the base of this lamp is eco-friendly, because it's made of fast-growing rubber wood.

- By using energy-efficient light bulbs, this lamp becomes even more green.

attention-getting way. An even more low-key approach to accent lighting might be in the foyer, where a favorite work of art hangs over a console table. A tabletop lamp that's sculptural in style might diffuse soft light over the area while keeping pace with the room's artistic spirit.

Lamps made of sustainable materials are on the rise, as are those created from recycled materials. The latter can even give a room a personal touch. What could be better, for instance, than a vintner's kitchen that features pendant lights made of recycled wine bottles?

Recycled

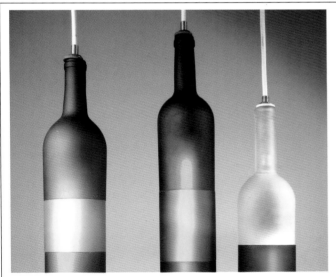

- Recycled bottles are hand-cut, reassembled, and polished to create these striped, sculptural-looking accent lamps.

- The number of colored sections per lamp varies, as do the colors themselves.

- Clear and green sections allow more light to shine through the pendant lamps, while darker brown sections dim the illumination.

- Fitted with a special low-wattage elongated bulb, the light source runs the length of the lamp itself.

Innovative

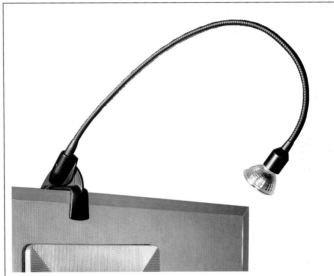

- Accent lights greatly enhance fine works of art, spotlighting them in the same way a museum or gallery would.

- The curved rod that supports this fixture's head can be adjusted to shine the light precisely where you need it most.

- Fitted with a small bulb, this fixture sheds more light than its size might seem.

171

LIGHTING

DECORATIVE LIGHTING

A decorative light or two in a room can add style and a green element, too.

Don't make the mistake of thinking that decorative lighting is nothing more than something pleasant to look at. Lamps and fixtures that fall under the decorative heading do double duty, not only fulfilling their general, task, or accent lighting purpose but also doing it in an aesthetically pleasing way.

Simple decorative lighting can, sometimes, be the most striking, which is precisely the tack that certain fixtures take. Milky-shaded cylinders, with energy-efficient LED bulbs, provide a soft glow similar to that of candles. But their beauty is more than skin deep; the portable lights are rechargeable, too, running a full eight hours per charge. Other lights, meanwhile, are more complex in pattern, but equally eye-

Energy-Efficient

- Some portable lights automatically light up when lifted from their charger and start charging again once they're put back.

- This type of light runs approximately eight hours before needing to be recharged.

- Providing a soft glow similar to that of a candle, one—or several—is a good choice at bedside or at the dining room table.

- The lights are illuminated by energy-efficient LED bulbs.

Sustainable

- Sustainably gathered cocoa leaves form the shade of this floor lamp.

- The leaves are fossilized— dried, hard-rubbed to remove the chlorophyll, and then stained with organic dyes.

- The shade is completely hand-stitched and hand-band, making it even more eco-friendly.

- The frame is made of durable wrought iron and the legs are made of sustainable bamboo.

catching. You'll find decorative lamps that feature shades made of shells that have washed onto the shore. By cross-cutting the sustainably gathered shells, they're transformed into pieces that allow light to shine through and, at the same time, expose the shells' inner intricacies.

In fact, there's practically no end to the number of items that are being recycled into decorative lighting. If a material is nonflammable, it's bound to show up in some type of lamp. Who knew that even postconsumer chopsticks could have an ornamental purpose?

Recycled

- Discarded traffic lights are recycled brilliantly in this type of pendant lamp.

- Available in both 8-inch and 12-inch diameters, the lights come (of course) in red, yellow, and green.

- The simple fixture can be used alone or in multiples for a dramatic effect.

- This pendant light comes with a low-voltage bulb, but is LED compatible, too.

Innovative

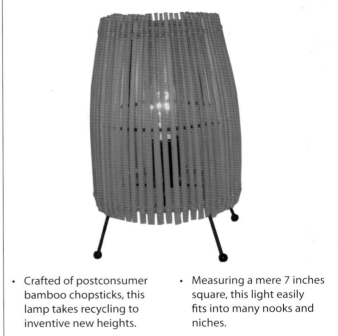

- Crafted of postconsumer bamboo chopsticks, this lamp takes recycling to inventive new heights.

- The chopsticks can be aligned in a straight manner, creating a geometric shape, or slightly bent for one that's more organic.

- Measuring a mere 7 inches square, this light easily fits into many nooks and niches.

- Though Asian inspired, it's a good fit with any decor.

LIGHTING

LIGHT BULBS

Using an energy-saving bulb costs very little but makes a big impact on the environment.

The right light bulb can make an enormous difference on the environment. Each time you replace one that's burned out, you can make a smaller carbon footprint. By substituting an energy-saving CFL for a standard incandescent, for instance, you'll use approximately 75 percent less energy, which translates to thirty dollars in savings over the life of the bulb. If ev-

ery U.S. household replaced just one standard light bulb with a CFL, it would prevent enough pollution to equal removing one million cars from the road.

LEDs are now being used more, too. Until recently, these energy-efficient, solid light bulbs were limited to single-bulb use in applications such as instrument panels and electron-

Compact Fluorescents

- Compared to standard incandescents, CFLs typically use about 75 percent less energy and last up to ten times longer.

- CFL bulbs fit almost any light, but are best suited for open fixtures that allow airflow.

- While most CFLs provide warm or soft white light, those in cooler colors are better for task lighting.

- To choose the CFL with the right amount of light, find one that's labeled as the equivalent to the incandescent bulb you are replacing.

LED Bulbs

- LED bulbs last ten times as long as compact fluorescents, and more than one hundred times longer than typical incandescents.

- Because LED bulbs are solid and don't have a filament, they aren't as likely to break as incandescents.

- LED bulbs come in several colors, each with a specific purpose; white produces a soft white light without any harsh glare or shadows.

- Although costs continue to go down, LEDs are still relatively expensive.

ics. But new types of LED bulbs, grouped in clusters with diffuser lenses, are now being used in everyday items, such as lamps.

Specialty bulbs are available, too. Halogen, for instance, has a clear, bright light, but it takes some careful handling. It's important to use a clean rag to handle a halogen bulb, because the oil from your skin will cause the bulb to burn hotter and, in turn, reduce its longevity. Full-spectrum bulbs are becoming increasingly popular, too. Simply put, this type of bulb replicates the light that you'd get from sunshine.

ZOOM

Not sure what kind of energy-efficient bulb is best for your lamp or fixture? Go to www.edf.org, where you will find recommendations for bulbs that match your criteria. You'll also find pictures of each type, so you will know what to look for when you go to the store.

Halogen

- Halogen lights use the same technology as incandescent bulbs, but last up to three times longer and produce almost 50 percent more light.

- This type of bulb produces a bright, pure light, making close-up tasks easier.

- Halogen bulbs are more expensive than incandescents and have a higher heat output, which increases the risk of a fire.

- Because halogen bulbs burn very hot, allow them to cool completely before changing.

Full-Spectrum Bulbs

- Full-spectrum bulbs are often referred to as daylight bulbs, as they contain Neodymium in the glass, which emits clear, white light that simulates the color of sunlight at noon.

- Its crisp, clear light is well suited to close-up tasks.

- This type of light bulb can last up to twenty thousand hours, about seven times as long as an incandescent.

- This type of light is a good choice for those who suffer from seasonal affective disorder (SAD).

LIGHTING

ALL THE EXTRAS

The right accessories can make your energy-efficient light fixtures even more so.

In addition to making smart decisions about light fixtures and bulbs, there are more energy-conscious steps that you can take. Dimmers are one of the most obvious ways to control the amount of voltage that your lights use. You'll find a wide variety today, but be sure to research your options thoroughly, as different types (and amounts) of light require different systems. And while there are still manual timers—those that you plug directly into the wall, then plug the light fixture into the dimmer—technology has given them a boost, too. Some timers even control multiple lights from a single wall unit.

The amount of energy that incandescent and halogen bulbs use can be dialed back with a simple socket adaptor,

Dimmer Switches

- Dimmer types include those suitable for standard line voltage (600W), high wattage (1000W–2000W), low-voltage magnetic (inductive), and low-voltage electronic (solid state).

- Dimmers let you control the amount of light used, thus energy costs, too.

- Some dimmers have preset capabilities, allowing you to establish a primary light level, then quickly change it to a second preset level.

- Most dimmers power the light gradually instead of closing the circuit instantly, which ultimately lengthens the life of the light.

Timers

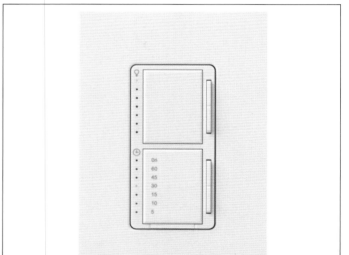

- Timers provide another way to control the amount of light you use, and in what rooms.

- Electronic timers installed in place of a switch plate can have multiple preset buttons, allowing you to control a variety of lights and appliances.

- Some electronic wall timers feature a time-delay switch, allowing lights to stay on for several minutes before they shut off.

- Manual timers plug directly into the wall, with lights plugging into them and turning on and off at specified times.

too. This small device, which attaches to the end of a bulb's socket, can triple a bulb's longevity while saving a good 10 percent in energy. But to keep an eye on the amount of energy that all of your home's lights and appliances consume, consider getting a monitor that will help you track usage right down to the kilowatt-hour. You can quickly and easily calculate electricity costs—and just may be surprised to find out which items in your home are most efficient and which ones aren't.

Socket Adaptors

- A socket adaptor uses microchip technology to control the voltage that a bulb receives.

- While the visible light level remains the same, the 10 percent energy savings increases the bulb's life approximately 300 percent.

- These adaptors work with incandescent and halogen bulbs up to 100 watts, and they're dimmable, too.

- Unfortunately, socket adaptors do not work with CFLs, LEDs, or three-way lamps.

Electricity-Use Monitors

- This type of monitor reveals how much electricity a light or appliance uses.

- After plugging your item into the monitor, energy consumption is measured by the kilowatt-hour, in much the same way that utility companies do.

- The monitor displays volts, amps, and watts, allowing you to estimate electricity costs by the hour, the week, the month, and even the year.

- It's a quick and easy way to find out which items are energy efficient, and which ones aren't.

LIGHTING

FOR THE LIVING ROOM
Even the smallest decorative touches in the living room can be green.

Take a look around your living room. How many of your accessories are green? The truth is, almost everything can be environmentally friendly to some degree, whether it's made of sustainable materials or recycled in some way.

Decorative screens, for instance, can be both functional and aesthetically pleasing—creating a cozy room-within-a-room or serving as a stunning backdrop. And so much the better if the screen is made of a sustainable material such as bamboo. Its inherent neutral hue gives a piece made of bamboo flexibility, too, making it a good fit for any room of the house.

Bowls and bottles can have that same kind of adaptability. In the living room, these types of finishing touches can take

Sustainable Bamboo

- A decorative screen can divide a large room into two smaller spaces, or serve as a backdrop, softening a corner of a room.

- This one, made of eco-friendly bamboo, is flexible enough to be twisted and turned into various forms.

- It's easy to roll up for storage or to move from room to room.

- A nontoxic, water-based finish allows the bamboo's natural hue to come through.

Recycled Metal

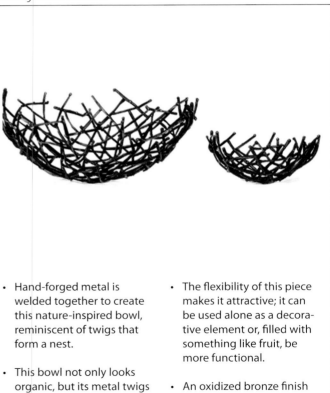

- Hand-forged metal is welded together to create this nature-inspired bowl, reminiscent of twigs that form a nest.

- This bowl not only looks organic, but its metal twigs are recycled, too.

- The flexibility of this piece makes it attractive; it can be used alone as a decorative element or, filled with something like fruit, be more functional.

- An oxidized bronze finish gives this bowl an attractive, aged character.

center stage on a coffee table, especially if they're oversize, which gives them a commanding presence. Some can serve double duty, too. A bowl, for instance, can hold everything from apples to small collectibles, while a bottle can be called into service as a vase.

Even the flowers you buy to freshen a room can be organic. If you have a green thumb, grow your own without the use of any pesticides. If you don't, ask your florist for those that are certified Veriflora™—the floral industry's first social and environmental standard.

Eco-Conscious Glass

- Whether set on a shelf or a coffee table, decorative bottles like this one can be an eye-catching focal point.

- Even the graceful form of this teardrop-shaped bottle has an organic look.

- Available in two heights and various colors, each of these handmade bottles is crafted of recycled glass.

- Taking the green strategy one step further, the glass itself is processed in an electric furnace that's powered by wind energy.

Organic Flowers

- Organic flowers come from growers that are committed to high environmental standards.

- They're grown and harvested using practices in which the goal is to improve the quality of farm working conditions and minimize damage to ecosystems.

- Organic flowers are always handpicked and shipped fresh to their destination.

- To guarantee their origin, look for flowers that are marked as Veriflora™, the country's first social and environmental certification standard for the floral industry.

FOR THE DINING ROOM

Glassware can make your dining room more eco-friendly, but there are other options, too.

The dining room is one of the easiest places to go green. Team up a sustainable wood table with a set of recycled chairs, and you're well on your way. Add an all-wool rug and some eco-friendly storage and you'll have made another big stride. But don't overlook the details, either. Glass dinnerware is a good place to start. It's sturdy enough to be used every day but striking enough for special meals, too. Additionally, it's completely recyclable, which is why there are so many table settings made of recycled glass. Serving pieces made of glass are a natural, as well, but also consider other eco-friendly materials, including sustainable wood—even those that are relatively unknown, such as kiri.

Recycled Glass

- Recycled glass dinnerware—in a single color or mixed and matched—brings an eco-friendly element to any meal.

- The bright colors have a shimmering quality, making it attractive for dining and as everyday accents, too.

- Recycled glass is sturdy enough that it can be put in the dishwasher.

- Its green qualities are long lasting; if you break the glassware, it can be recycled again.

Sustainable Wood

- Hand-carved from the discarded root balls of Chinese fir trees, these bowls can be used for fruit and centerpieces, or stand alone as sculptural works of art.

- Because these bowls are untreated, cracks can eventually occur, making them inappropriate for liquids of any kind.

- All that's needed to keep the wood moist and beautiful is an occasional rubbing with food-grade oil.

A green centerpiece might include a vase made of glass, ceramic, or even recycled paper or felt. The ultimate in portability, some paper vases pop open whenever and wherever you need them, ready to hold your favorite flowers. When no longer needed, simply disassemble them and put them away until needed again. And innovative vases made of felt are lined to be watertight. Even something as simple as a green plant can make a stunning centerpiece. It becomes more attractive, too, when set in a carefully chosen, eco-friendly container.

Biodegradable Paper

- The ultimate in portability, this vase pops open to display flowers when and where you need it and then folds up again when you no longer need it.

- This biodegradable vase can be used over and over again.

- Made of recycled-content paper, this vase is waterproof, thanks to a thin laminate coating on the inside.

Natural Plants

- Air plants, which include some orchids, don't need soil in which to grow, because they derive their nutrition from air and water.

- This particular air plant garden, an easy-to-care-for centerpiece, is set in a bed of smooth white river stones.

- The planter itself is a soapstone baker, which can later be used in the kitchen.

- The soapstone piece has the ability to go directly from the oven to table.

FOR THE BEDROOM

Nontoxic materials are important in a room where you spend a good third of your time.

Eco-friendly accessories in the bedroom are just as important as environmentally safe furnishings. Think of it in terms of how much time you spend in the room. Do you really want to breathe in toxic fumes eight hours a day?

Recycled pieces are a great place to start. Vintage accents, as well as hand-me-down family favorites—if more than just a few years old—will have had plenty of time for any toxic fumes they may have had originally to dissipate. Or, consider new accessories made of recycled materials. Every thing you can possibly imagine is being recycled today, and some that you may not imagine at all. Paper egg cartons, for instance, are being transformed into comfy footstools. Even pieces of

Recycled Paper

- This footstool is handmade from 100 percent recycled paper-pulp egg cartons.

- Water-based fabric dye gives the piece its color, and no varnish or lacquer has been used.

- The footstool can be used upright or on its side to create a rocking motion; upright, it can also be used as a sturdy base for a glass-top coffee table.

- To clean, all that's needed is a light vacuuming.

Reclaimed Wood

- Versatile baskets, set on top of a chest or dresser, are a good choice to corral small items in any bedroom.

- Made of driftwood, the basket above is a departure from traditional woven pieces.

- The pieces of surf- and sand-smoothed driftwood used to make this container was found along the beach.

- Because they're watertight, baskets like this can be used to stash small items or as planters.

driftwood that wash up on the beach are being reclaimed to create elements of home decor.

It goes without saying, too, that finishing touches made of natural materials are, well, a natural. And if they're handmade instead of machine made, so much the better. Decorative throw pillows are readily available in wool, linen, hemp, and organic cotton. Their colors and patterns make them appealing, but look beneath the covers, too. Fillings should be just as natural, whether they're organic cotton, pure wool, or even silky kapok. If the natural materials in your accessories are renewable, you will have an even greener room. Sustainable bamboo is an increasingly popular option, but there are also lesser-known alternatives such as water hyacinth. With a look similar to that of wicker, it can be woven in much the same way, too. Likewise, it's a chameleon of sorts, with the ability to blend into any room scheme.

Natural Hemp

- Pillows with coverings made of 100 percent hemp are extremely durable and have a look that's similar to linen.

- Hemp is fire- and mold-resistant, and continues to soften with repeated washings.

- The pillows are filled with a mixture of recycled poly-cotton and scrap foam that would otherwise be send to a landfill.

- Even the dyes used in these pillows are eco-friendly, made with flowers, leaves, seeds, and bark.

Renewable Hyacinth

- This multipurpose piece works as well as an end table as it does an extra seating piece.

- The design of the piece allows the drawer, when closed, to be all but invisible.

- It's made of handwoven water hyacinth wrapped around a rattan frame, materials that are both natural and durable.

- Water hyacinth is a highly renewable natural fiber that grows quickly in parts of Asia.

FOR THE BATHROOM

Green tactics in the bath can be practical and appealing to the eye, as well.

By their very nature, bathrooms should be sparkling clean but, at the same time, they can be just as green. Decorative accents that are environmentally friendly are readily available, starting with the towel bars, hooks, and toilet paper holders found throughout the room. Forged iron, for example, doesn't require a finish of any kind. It's being used to create pieces

that go far beyond the material's traditional roots, showing up in contemporary forms, as well. Likewise, the knobs and pulls you put on your cabinetry can be green. Forged iron hardware is a good choice here, too, but also consider the vast range of colors you can add with knobs and pulls made of glass.

GREEN DECORATING & REMODELING

Durable Metal

- A bathroom's towel bars, hooks, and toilet paper holders can be as green as any thing else in the room.

- This towel bar, inspired by nature, is hand forged of recycled iron.

- Like leaves themselves, no two hand-forged pieces are alike, because they're hammered and shaped by blacksmiths.

- Recycled iron like this is durable enough to last for years but can eventually be recycled again.

Recycled Glass

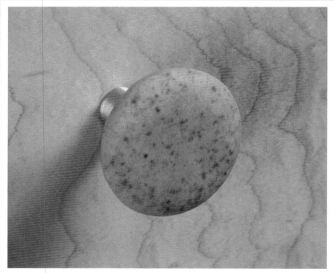

- New knobs and pulls are an inexpensive way to update bathroom cabinetry and can be changed in a matter of minutes.

- Featuring recycled glass, knobs and pulls can add an instant splash of color.

- Glass is a good choice for the bath, because it's easy to wipe down with the rest of the room.

- Glass knobs also have the advantage of being recyclable again.

No bathroom is complete without at least a touch of luxury, and one place to start is with bath salts. Those made of organic materials are not only better for the environment but also better for your body. Often scented with essential oils, they naturally soothe muscles that are stiff and sore. While going through your bathroom routine, it's nice to have a place to sit down, too. Whether you have room for only a small stool or your space can accommodate a longer bench, look for those made of materials such as bamboo that are up to green standards.

GREEN ● LIGHT

There's something luxurious about taking a bath by candlelight. Look for candles made of soy wax that are clean burning and made from a renewable resource. Scented with pure essential oils, this type of candle is long lasting, sometimes with up to forty hours of burn time.

Natural Sea Salt

- Bath salts, which come in varieties from fine to coarse, provide a natural way to ease stiff, sore muscles.

- With the addition of Epsom salt, Hawaiian sea salts like these are good for exfoliating, too.

- Fragrances are added with pure essential oils such as lavender and rose, adding an element of aromatherapy.

- Even these containers, vintage milk bottles, are environmentally friendly.

Sustainable Bamboo

- A place to sit while getting dressed in the morning is essential in any bathroom, and green options are plentiful.

- These simple stools, made of bamboo, are durable and sustainable.

- The 30-inch-wide stools provide plenty of comfort, and bathtowels can be stacked below.

- These contemporary seating pieces come in natural, cherry, and ebony finishes—all of which are nontoxic.

FOR THE KITCHEN

In the kitchen, make good green choices and get into good composting habits.

If you're eco-conscious enough to buy only organic foods, why would you cook and serve them with anything that's less than green? The kitchen towels and potholders you use, for instance, can be made of one of the most environmentally friendly fibers—hemp. It naturally disperses heat well and is strong enough to stand up to tough, everyday use. Bamboo, too, is being used in a wide variety of ways, for everything from dish towels to cutting boards. It's particularly appealing in the form of dinnerware, whether left in its natural, caramel color or given a brighter hue.

Also take time to think about how your kitchen is used on a daily basis. If your family tends to open the refrigerator of-

GREEN DECORATING & REMODELING

Natural Hemp

- Because hemp disperses heat well, it's a good choice for potholders and oven mitts.

- Hemp is one of the strongest and most durable textile fibers, giving it the ability to stand up to everyday use.

- The linen-like fabric also takes color well, so you'll find items made of hemp in a variety of deep hues.

- Hemp is machine washable, and becomes softer with each use.

Sustainable Bamboo

- Bamboo is not only being used for furniture and floors; it's also being used to create a variety of kitchen wares, including plates, bowls, and eating utensils.

- Bamboo is lightweight yet stronger than some hardwoods.

- These colorful salad bowls, made from the renewable material, are durable and food-safe for cold and hot dishes alike.

- All it takes to clean bamboo dinnerware is a little soap and warm water.

ten to reach for a favorite beverage, consider a countertop container for water or any beverages that are just as tasty at room temperature. A beverage dispenser can be set on top of the counter in one corner of the kitchen, eliminating the energy lost each time the fridge door is opened. And be sure to save room for a countertop composting unit. If it's conveniently close, you're more apt to get in the habit of tossing the appropriate items in—and have more compost for your garden.

Glass

- Countertop drink dispensers allow family members to pour their beverages without repeatedly opening and closing the refrigerator door.

- This one is made of recycled glass that gives it a vintage look.

- It's set on a handcrafted metal base that raises the dispenser up from the countertop, allowing easy access to the spigot.

- Dispensers like this one are perfect for the patio or other outdoor eating areas, too.

Containing Compost

- A composting crock set on the kitchen countertop makes the everyday task convenient.

- This crock's glazed interior won't stain and holds up to a full gallon of kitchen scraps.

- To prevent odors from escaping, the lid is fitted with a carbon filter that lasts up to three months.

- Less than 11 inches high and 7 inches in diameter, this composting crock takes up very little countertop space.

FOR THE KID'S ROOM

Toys and other kids' stuff can be just as eco-friendly as it is safe.

There's no doubt that kids' rooms, and their contents, corner the market on "cute." What's impressive, though, is just how many of these endearing items can be eco-friendly, too. You'll find stuffed animals made of recycled sweaters that are cuddly and, equally important, can be thrown right into the washer. And many of the softest kids' blankets are made of recycled materials, too. Some, in fact, have patterns that are so imaginative that you'll be tempted to hang them on the wall like artwork—or even use them as a throw yourself.

Clocks can be just as functional as they are fun, whether they're made of natural materials or those that have been re-purposed for a new lease on life. There's something appropri-

Plush Toys

- Because children, especially young ones, have a propensity to put things in their mouths, it's important that their toys be nontoxic.

- These stuffed animals are made from recycled sweaters and filled with shredded recycled polyester.

- Eco-friendly down to the last detail, even this penguin's bill and feet are made of soft cotton jersey.

- Although they're not machine washable, these plush toys can be gently hand washed.

Wall Art

- Wall art in a child's room can be just as eco-friendly as any other decorative element.

- This graphic piece is made of hemp/organic cotton that's been stretched onto a wooden frame.

- Each piece is silkscreened by hand with eco-friendly, water-based dyes.

- This print is part of a larger collection, which also includes organic pillows and blankets in coordinating patterns.

ately childlike, for instance, about a clock with a chalkboard face made of eco-friendly slate. With all of these sustainable items for kids, however, sooner or later you'll probably face a storage shortage of some kind. Simple baskets are one way to go, but also consider freestanding, locker-style units that are just as suitable for kids in elementary school as they are for those in college. Designs that are durable and have that kind of long-lasting appeal are right in step with the green way of thinking.

GREEN ● LIGHT

Picture frames seem to find their way into any kid's room, showing off photos of your children or their artwork. There are plenty of eco-friendly frame options, including those made of various recycled items. But if safety is a concern, look for those made of hemp or paper that have no glass at all.

Natural Slate

- Wall clocks are convenient in a child's room, whether to time naps or teach time-reading skills.

- This one is made of natural slate, its chalkboard-like face allowing kids to create their own numerals.

- The two pendulums hold chalk and the cloth that can wipe the slate clean, both of which can be detached via their snap hooks.

- This clock operates quietly on a single AA battery.

Versatile Lockers

- Freestanding lockers can add supplemental storage in kids' rooms, where there's seemingly never enough.

- Built from recycled steel, this locker contains a bar to hang clothes from and a built-in shelf.

- The lockers' bright colors are appealing to kids, and they're easy to wipe down, too.

- These lockers are versatile enough to grow up with your child, and even make the move to a dorm room.

BEDS

Comfortable, nontoxic sleeping spots are as important for pets as they are for their owners.

When it comes to needing a nontoxic environment, pets are no different than people. They require a healthy atmosphere, and that starts with their sleeping spots. With the wide variety of pet products available today, there's seemingly no end to bed options for dogs. But when it comes to being eco-friendly, simple styles are often the best. There are those, for instance, that have natural-fiber covers colored with low-impact dyes and filled with nontoxic materials, too. And some sleeping pads go the next step by utilizing recycled plastic bottles as their primary material.

Feline quarters, as well, are quite conducive to being green. The ultimate in kitty quarters may be "condos," some outfit-

Dog Beds

- Today's dog beds range in style from simple round pillows or mattresses to elaborate pieces of furniture.

- One of the best options remains the most basic, like this dog bed made of 100 percent cotton denim.

- This eco-friendly sleeping spot uses low-impact dyes and is filled with organic kapok, a silky fiber obtained from the kapok tree.

- The zippered cover is easily removed for machine washing.

Sleeping Pads

- Because it's thinner and more lightweight, a sleeping pad is easily portable from place to place.

- This earth-friendly product, made from postconsumer recycled plastic soda bottles, is versatile, too; it can also be used to line a carrier or crate.

- Both the outer fabric and the inner fill of this sleeping spot are nontoxic and hypoallergenic.

- These beda, both durable and reversible, are machine washable, too.

ted with several levels to climb and built-in scratching posts, too. The best of the bunch are nontoxic and use materials that include wood, recycled cardboard, hemp, and organic cotton batting. If you really want to pamper your cat, include a suspended felt toy or two. For true climbers, consider a cat tree, something for your pet to scratch other than the furniture. You'll find them in all kinds of shapes and sizes, some of them strikingly contemporary. Most important, though, look for those made of eco-friendly materials such as recycled cardboard and nontoxic paints.

Cat Condos

- The right kind of housing is important for pets of any kind to keep them secure, safe, and sound.

- Houses should be nontoxic and as natural as possible, like this cat condo made of recycled cardboard, wood, hemp, and organic cotton batting.

- For cats, keep in mind that they like to climb and have the ability to hide.

- Other popular options for felines include some kind of scratching post and small toys to bat at.

Cat Trees

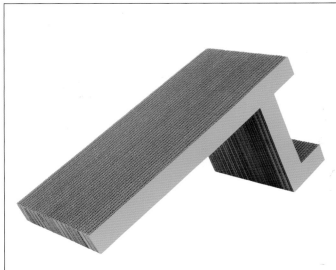

- A cat tree provides a place for felines to satisfy their penchant for scratching, instead of using the furniture.

- This version is made of 100 percent corrugated cardboard, more than a third of which is recycled.

- The surface is coated with no-VOC (volatile organic compound) paint, and the adhesives are nontoxic, too.

- The corrugated surface can be lightly sanded to conceal scratch marks.

COLLARS

Pet collars come in a wide assortment of natural and recycled materials.

A good collar is more than a fashion accent for your pet. It provides a place to snap on a leash as well as those all-important ID tags. The right one for your dog or cat, of course, depends on the size of your pet. A large dog might break a collar that's too thin or lightweight, while small cats and dogs don't need to carry around a heavy collar.

One of the most eco-friendly materials used for pet collars is hemp. This natural fiber is lightweight but, at the same time, strong and durable, making it a good match for pets large and small. Plus, hemp is hypoallergenic, so even dogs and cats with sensitive skin will find it comfortable. Like hemp, collars made of all cotton are soft against a pet's skin. Typi-

Hemp

Cotton

- Dog collars made of hemp have a heavy-duty, canvas-like construction.

- Some hemp collars are fitted with quick-release hardware (which unlatch if your pet gets caught on something) and are machine-washable and -dryable.

- Because hemp softens with age, these collars are extremely comfortable and get more so over time.

- Hemp is hypoallergenic, so it is particularly good for pets with sensitive skin.

- Collars made of cotton are readily available, but look for those that are all cotton versus those made of cotton and nylon.

- Cotton pet collars are lightweight and extremely durable.

- Because they are light-weight, and not as strong as some other fibers, all-cotton collars are best suited to cats and small dogs.

- Cotton fibers readily absorb dyes, so you will find cotton collars in a variety of colors.

cally, though, this type of collar isn't as strong, so it's best reserved for cats and small dogs.

It's not unusual, either, to find pet collars made of a wide variety of recycled materials. Some are being created from recycled inner tubes. Even a retired silk necktie can be transformed into a collar and matching leash. And some pet collars are infused with herbal oils, too. What better way to keep your pet smelling fresh?

Recycled

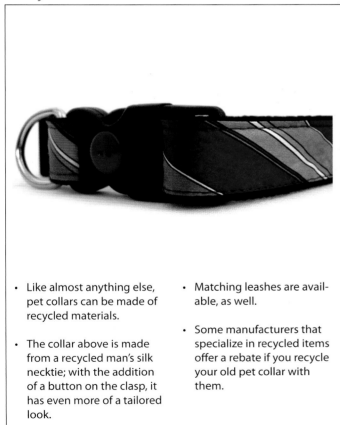

- Like almost anything else, pet collars can be made of recycled materials.

- The collar above is made from a recycled man's silk necktie; with the addition of a button on the clasp, it has even more of a tailored look.

- Matching leashes are available, as well.

- Some manufacturers that specialize in recycled items offer a rebate if you recycle your old pet collar with them.

MAKE IT EASY

If your cat spends time outdoors, put a bell on his collar. Not only will you be able to hear where he is, but the birds in the neighborhood will know, too! You can find bells in various colors and with reflective coatings, so you can see your pet in the dark.

Herbal

- Some pet collars, referred to as "scent collars," have herbal oils infused right into them.

- The natural blend of aromatic herbs, with a fresh mint fragrance, contains no harmful chemicals at all.

- A herbal collar is environmentally safe and will keep your pet smelling fresh.

- This type of collar is available for both dogs and cats.

193

TOYS

Pet toys aren't just for play but have a practical side, too.

Whether you realize it or not, the toys you buy for your pet can have real benefits. Depending on the type you choose, toys can relieve boredom (keeping them out of trouble), take the focus off of chewing the furniture, and even provide interactive play, strengthening the connection between you and your pet.

Recycled toys are particularly eco-friendly and can take many forms, repurposing a particular material to make something new. Some materials are recycled after exhausting their original purpose, but there are also examples of "immediate" recycling, like companies that use leftover plastic from first-run toys, regrinding it right away to make "recycled" ones.

Cotton Toys

- Considering how much time toys are in a pet's mouth, those made of all-natural materials such as cotton and wool are good choices.

- This cat toy is wrapped in durable cotton canvas.

- To make this throw toy even more enticing, it's filled with organic catnip.

- The lightweight, four-inch-square toy easily slides across the floor.

Hemp Toys

- The inherent strength and durability of hemp makes it a natural choice for pet toys, because it can stand up to daily wear and tear.

- The stuffed toys above feature a hemp canvas shell and filling made of recycled poly-cotton.

- Because hemp accepts dye well, these toys come in a variety of colors.

- Hemp is machine washable, becoming softer over time, and is biodegradable.

Cat toys can be as simple as small squares that they can hold between their paws or bat across the floor. And if they're filled with catnip—preferably of the organic variety—that's so much the better. You'll find these toys in cotton as well as hemp, the latter of which is being used increasingly for pet toys all the time. Hemp's inherent strength and durability makes it a natural choice; it stands up well to daily wear and tear. But you can feel good about choosing cat and dog toys made of any organic material. You'll be doing your pet—and the planet—a favor.

ZOOM

Toys made of natural rubber are fun for dogs to play with and a dental aid, too. They can give a dog's gums a workout and even prevent tartar from building up on the teeth. Some even have places to insert treats, which can keep a pet busy for hours.

Organic Toys

- Made of organic material, these plush toys are completely eco-friendly.

- The natural fibers are dyed with natural extracts from plants—the beige color, for instance, comes from chestnut bur, yellow from gardenia seed, and red from the madder root.

- The natural dyes are set with nothing more than a pure water wash.

- These toys have removable squeakers, which can be taken out before each machine washing.

Recycled Toys

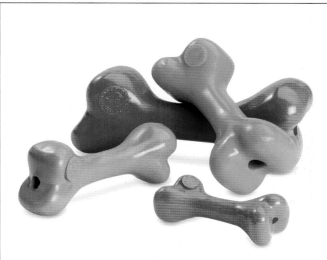

- These recycled bones are made from "regrind"—material left over after the company's made their first-quality chew toys.

- This manufacturing process ensures that every ounce of the material gets used.

- Best of all, the chew toy can be recycled again sometime in the future.

- Other recycled options include tug toys made of preconsumer recycled fire hose cloth.

BOWLS

The bowls that you use for your pets should be just as safe as the food they eat.

You wouldn't eat off just any plate, especially if it were laden with toxic finishes. So why would you serve up your pet's dinner with anything that's subpar? There's a wide variety of options at your disposal, one for every style preference and size of breed.

Stainless steel bowls are one of the most basic types,

popular for their durability and their light weight. In fact, if you find them so lightweight that your pet keeps pushing dinner across the floor, look for styles that have a strip of rubber around the bottom to keep them from slipping. Ceramic bowls are a heavier option, and they're available in a virtual rainbow of colors and even more patterns. More than

Metal

- Bowls made of stainless steel are durable enough for heavy-duty, everyday use.

- Stainless steel will not rust, crack, or discolor in any way.

- One of the least expensive options, stainless steel bowls don't retain odors and are easy to keep clean.

- Some stainless steel pet bowls come with a thin rubber strip around the bottom to keep them from skidding across the floor.

Ceramic

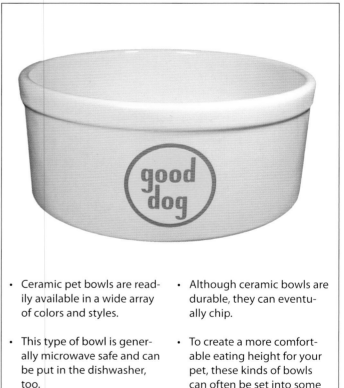

good dog

- Ceramic pet bowls are readily available in a wide array of colors and styles.

- This type of bowl is generally microwave safe and can be put in the dishwasher, too.

- Although ceramic bowls are durable, they can eventually chip.

- To create a more comfortable eating height for your pet, these kinds of bowls can often be set into some kind of raised feeder.

anything else, however, be sure that your pet's ceramic bowls have lead-free glazes.

For cats and small dogs, food dishes of any kind can be placed directly on the floor. But medium-size and large dogs often benefit from raised feeders that bring their food and water up to a more comfortable level. If you're concerned about the purity of the water you're giving your pet, consider an electric fountain that can aerate and filter it. After all, nothing's too good for these four-legged members of the family.

ZOOM

For pets on the go, try travel bowls that are lightweight, durable, and eco-friendly, too. Those made of Eco Tex™, a tightly woven poly blend fabric created from recycled plastic soda bottles, is waterproof. They're completely collapsible, too, so you can pack them flat, then pop them up when you're ready to use.

Feeders

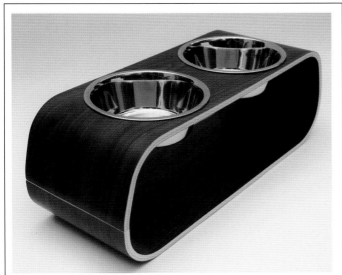

- Raised feeders can be simple or sophisticated; this contemporary version is a little of both.

- The clean-lined piece is crafted from a single piece of plywood, utilizing a bentwood process.

- Wood that's been steam bent can yield eight to ten times more usable wood from a log than solid lumber.

- Stainless steel bowls lift out for cleaning, and the seamless feeder can be wiped down easily, too.

Waterers

- Electric drinking fountains can filter and aerate water, keeping it fresher than a bowl of standing water.

- Because the water is continuously moving and aerated with healthy oxygen, it cools naturally, too.

- This fountain is fitted with a charcoal filter that gets rid of bad odors and tastes.

- This unit, which disassembles for easy cleaning, works for both cats and dogs.

TOWELS AND MATS

Pet towels and mats may seem inconsequential, but the right ones can make a big day-to-day difference.

Whether your pet has just come inside after roaming your property or had a bath, you'll need to have a thick towel on hand to clean up and wipe down. All-cotton towels are a logical choice. They're durable and absorbent, plus they can stand up to repeated washings. But look beyond the conventional choices to those specifically made for pets. One type has pockets sewn into the corners, allowing you to get a better grip before rubbing down your dog. But if it's more absorbency you're looking for, consider towels made of bamboo. It's one of the strongest fibers you'll find.

Cleanliness is a factor in other ways, too. To keep things tidy at dinnertime, put a food mat under you cat's or dog's

Cotton Towels

- Towels used specifically for drying off your dog need to be superabsorbent.

- This one is made of terry cloth woven from rugged, heavyweight cotton.

- With pockets built into all four corners, you can hold your dog with one hand and dry with the other without getting wet.

- While this towel is made expressly for drying a dog, standard all-cotton towels are a good choice, too.

Bamboo Towels

- Because bamboo is even more absorbent than cotton, towels made of this fiber are good to use on pets, too.

- Bamboo is an extremely strong fiber, durable enough for your four-legged friends.

- Bamboo is naturally antibacterial.

- Towels made of 100 percent bamboo are available in limited colors, while those that combine bamboo and cotton come in a broader range.

bowls—especially if your pet tends to be a sloppy eater. It's a lot easier to clean up a mat than the floor itself. Likewise, it's important to have a mat next to the litter box. By their very nature, cats will look for a place to wipe their paws, to get rid of any excess litter, so provide a dedicated place to make it easier for you and your pet. It's the little things that can make a big difference, each and every day.

Food Mats

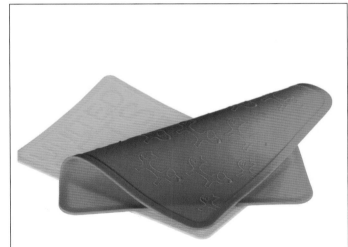

- Feeding mats protect a floor from food and water spills, an especially good idea if your pet is an enthusiastic eater.

- This mat, made of nonslip rubber, holds firmly to the floor while keeping bowls securely in place.

- The 18-square-inch size easily accommodates a pair of bowls.

- The rubber material is not only extremely durable but easy to wipe clean, as well.

Litter Mats

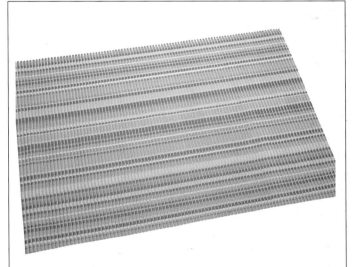

- Cats need to have a place where they can wipe off their feet next to their litter boxes.

- This colorful mat traps excess litter. Its soft surface opens up the cat's paws to dislodge any litter or dirt without harming the paws themselves.

- The mat has two important attributes—it's easy to clean and durable.

- It's large enough to fit completely under a litter box, but can be trimmed to a smaller size, too.

CLEANING UP

From head to toe, keep your pet clean in an eco-friendly way.

If you wash your pet once every week or two, think of all the chemicals that could potentially be going down the drain—and directly into the earth. By choosing and using natural products, you'll leave less of a carbon footprint and your four-legged friend will undoubtedly feel better, too.

All-natural shampoos, for instance, are available in every special formula you can imagine. Some are moisturizing, some are hypoallergenic, and some even deter pesky fleas. What's more, all that's used to fragrance these products are sweet-smelling essential oils. Between baths, use pet wipes that are just as chemical free. They're a quick and easy way to wash muddy paws, for instance.

Natural Shampoo

- Pet shampoos can be found in a wide variety of all-natural formulas.

- Look for those with ingredients specific to what your pet needs—shea butter moisturizes, for instance, while oatmeal soothes and lanolin hydrates dry, itchy skin.

- Essential oils such as orange, eucalyptus, tea tree, citronella, and rosemary can add fresh scents and naturally deter fleas.

- Natural shampoos are even safe for frequent washings.

Pet Wipes

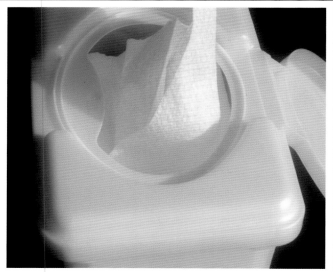

- Between baths, diminish dirt and odors with all-natural grooming wipes, good for everything from muddy paws to drool and dander.

- Wipes like these not only clean but have a conditioning element, too, leaving your pet with a shiny coat.

- Some wipes have a fragrance, provided by essential oils, while others are hypoallergenic and fragrance free.

- They're safe for even daily use for most cats and dogs.

Also keep the environment in mind when cleaning up after your dog or cat's waste. Kitty litter is available in all-natural forms, some of which use nothing more than pine pellets to neutralize odors and add fresh scents. Plus, biodegradable litter-pan liners and dog-waste bags, made primarily of cornstarch, can decompose in as little as ten days and are compostable, too. Needless to say, they're a huge improvement over the plastic bags that you may have been using, which can take well over a century to decompose.

Natural Kitty Litter

- All-natural kitty litters can do the job just as well as those that have chemicals.

- Litter made of Southern yellow pine, for instance, neutralizes odors and provides a pleasant scent, too.

- Once the pellets break down naturally, the boxful of litter can be emptied into a compost or mulching pile.

- Like any other variety, all-natural litters are available in both conventional and clumping types.

Biodegradable Bags

- Dog-waste bags that are made of plastic can take more than one hundred years to degrade; instead, look for bags that are completely biodegradable and compostable.

- Some types of bags, with cornstarch as the main ingredient, can decompose in as few as ten days, depending on the composting technique used.

- This type of biodegradable bag is available for dogs as well as kitty-litter pans.

NATURAL FURNITURE

Outdoor furniture made of natural materials can be comfortable and good for Mother Earth.

Furniture that's made of natural fibers blends beautifully into a back yard or a garden, becoming part of the landscape itself. Willow furniture, for example, has been around for years. Using the pliable branches of the willow tree, this kind of outdoor-friendly furniture can be made in a wide variety of shapely forms. Most people prefer that the bark be left on, but—for a lighter look—it can be stripped from the branches.

In addition to willow furniture, pieces made of sustainable natural fibers make up a large percentage of outdoor furniture. The category as a whole is often referred to as "wicker," but that's really a misnomer, because each natural fiber has

GREEN DECORATING & REMODELING

Willow

- Willow trees have pliable branches that can easily be shaped into various furniture forms.

- This type of wood is one of the few that will keep its bark, even after being cut.

- To retain the original beauty of the wood and protect it against the elements, apply a water sealer that contains boiled linseed oil.

- The wood will naturally crack as it dries out, but that won't affect its strength.

Rattan

- One of nature's strongest materials, rattan grows in the tropical forests of Asia.

- The outer skin of rattan pole is a form of wicker, but wicker can also be made from rush, cane, willow, and reed.

- Rattan doesn't splinter or break, and it bends well into various forms.

- Furniture made of natural rattan should be used only on protected patios, porches, or sun rooms; it will deteriorate over time if left out in the elements.

its own attributes. Rattan is strong and doesn't splinter or break, but it's particularly susceptible to weather; because it can deteriorate if left out in the rain, it's best suited for covered porches and patios. Several species of bamboo, on the other hand, adapt well to outdoor use. And furniture made of sea grass, which includes materials such as water hyacinth and banana leaves, is tightly woven, which makes it enduring, too. All three types have distinctly different appearances, yet the natural roots that they have in common let them work well together in the same space.

· · · · · · · · · · · · · YELLOW ● LIGHT · · · · · · · · · · ·

To extend the life of any natural-fiber outdoor furniture, keep it out of the rain—and even the bright sun—as much as possible; a sheltered porch or patio is a good location. Keep it clean with a moist cloth and a little mild soap but avoid getting the plant material too wet.

Bamboo

- Bamboo furniture is lightweight but sturdy and has a tough, woodlike surface.

- Because bamboo can grow at a rate of 2 inches per hour, it can be harvested every two to five years.

- If not treated correctly, bamboo furniture can be prone to wood-boring insects. Maintain it according to the manufacturer's instructions.

- There are many different species of bamboo, so choose one that is well suited to outdoor use.

Sea Grass

- Furniture made of natural sea grass is sturdy enough to be used indoors or out.

- Some sea grass pieces feature a mix of natural materials, like this chaise that incorporates both water hyacinth and banana leaves.

- The resulting surface is tightly woven and relatively smooth to the touch.

- Sea grass furniture is generally found in its natural color, but you'll find it in darker hues, too.

OUTDOOR LIVING

WOOD FURNITURE

When choosing outdoor furniture made of wood, look for species that are sustainable.

Various types of wood are used to create outdoor furniture. The best picks, though, are those that are eco-friendly—from fast-growing, renewable resources or grown in forests managed in a responsible way.

Cedar is a strong, rot-resistant wood And furniture made from this species is aromatic. It doesn't all have the familiar red tone, however. While Western Red cedar is certainly utilized to some degree, other types, such as Northern White cedar, are used for a fair share of outdoor furniture, too. All species, though, have one thing in common: They weather to a soft, silvery gray over time.

Perhaps lesser known, but equally viable, is furniture made

Cedar

- Cedar is exceptionally strong and rot-resistant, making it a good choice for outdoor furniture.

- This type of wood doesn't shrink or warp like many others do.

- Furniture can be made of Western Red cedar as well as Northern White cedar, both of which—when left untreated—weather to a soft silvery gray.

- Look for furniture made of cedar that's been sustainably harvested.

Eucalyptus

- Eucalyptus is exceptionally strong, resistant to decay, and fast growing, making it a renewable material.

- This type of wood looks similar to teak, but is a less-expensive option.

- Furniture made of eucalyptus needs to be treated with nothing more than a nontoxic tung-oil sealer.

- To be sure your furniture is the most eco-friendly, look for pieces made of wood certified by the Forest Stewardship Council (FSC).

of eucalyptus wood. This fast-growing wood is similar to teak in its appearance, but it costs a fraction of the price. Brazilian cherry, meanwhile, may sound exotic, and it has a rich look, but the beauty of this wood species is more than skin-deep. Its rock-solid character makes it a natural for outdoor furnishings. It doesn't require any kind of finish, either, though you may opt to give it a coat of linseed oil or nontoxic stain. Teak, however, is considered the ultimate in outdoor furniture. Though expensive, teak is worth the investment, as it can literally last for decades.

Brazilian Cherry

Teak

- Brazilian cherry has an inherently warm, rich look.

- This wood species can be left unfinished, coated with linseed oil, or given a coat of nontoxic stain.

- Furniture made of Brazilian cherry is durable enough to be set outside, but it's often stylish enough to be used indoors, too.

- The most eco-friendly pieces are made of wood grown in well-managed forests, in an environmentally responsible way.

- Teak, a densely grained wood, is highly resistant to rot, warping, and swelling.

- The natural oils found in teak act as a natural preservative, allowing furniture to last for decades.

- Over time, this wood develops a silvery-gray patina that can be left as is or revived with a little teak oil.

- Look for products made from trees grown on plantations that follow sustainable practices according to Chain of Custody certificates.

MORE FASHIONABLE FURNITURE

Whether it's brand new or a recycled find, outdoor furniture is increasingly eco-friendly.

With the increasing popularity of outdoor living rooms, there's also a greater need for stylish outdoor furniture. And some of the most handsome pieces, as it turns out, are those created with a high regard for the planet.

A perennially popular option is aluminum; it's durable and it doesn't rust. Tubular aluminum often translates best to con-

temporary styles, while cast- and wrought-aluminum pieces are, as a rule, more traditional. Some of today's most innovative examples, though, are ultramodern designs that use a single flat sheet of the metal, taking inventive forms. Wrought iron, on the other hand, tends to honor its traditional roots, harkening back to the time when the material was forged by

Aluminum

- Outdoor furniture made of aluminum is sturdy, doesn't rust, and is able to withstand daily wear and tear as well as all kinds of weather.

- There are three basic categories of aluminum furniture—tubular (the most lightweight), cast, and wrought.

- Cast and wrought aluminum are often used indoors, too, in such places as breakfast areas and solariums.

- Maintenance requires no more than soap and water and a once-a-year application of liquid wax.

Wrought Iron

- Originally crafted by blacksmiths, wrought iron is durable and one of the heaviest types of outdoor furniture.

- The majority of wrought-iron furniture has a black finish, although you'll also find forest green, white, and various other colors.

- Quality wrought-iron pieces have a rust-resistant finish.

- Like aluminum, wrought iron should be cleaned with soap and water and given an annual application of wax.

blacksmiths. Even though the designs remain classic, however, the color palette has expanded beyond black. You're just as likely to find wrought iron in hues such as forest green and white.

If there's a variety of style among the assorted metals, there's even more so in furniture crafted of reclaimed or recycled items. Imagine sitting on chairs made from the reclaimed staves of wine barrels or relaxing on a seating piece created from recycled milk containers.

ZOOM

If you're considering metal furniture, first-generation aluminum and wrought iron aren't your only choices. Both aluminum and wrought iron can also be found in recycled forms, putting just a little less stress on the environment. What's more, the difference isn't even discernable to the naked eye.

OUTDOOR LIVING

Reclaimed

- Wine barrels are being reclaimed and repurposed in a wide variety of ways; they're sturdy and have an aged character that's appealing.

- This folding chair, for instance, is handcrafted of staves taken from barrels made of white oak.

- A natural linseed oil finish allows the wood to age beautifully, whether used indoors or out.

- The chair is easily portable, too, folding up to form a slim profile.

Recycled

- Some of the most innovative options in outdoor furniture are pieces made from unexpected materials such as recycled milk jugs.

- The plastic containers are broken down into pellets which, in turn, are transformed into "plastic lumber."

- The resulting durable material is impervious to all types of weather.

- This recycled type of furniture comes in traditional colors as well as those that are bright and bold.

RUGS

Rugs conducive to the outdoors can be just as green as their surroundings.

Furnishings intended for outdoor living don't stop at chairs and tables anymore. People are spending more time outside. As a result, they want their outdoor living rooms to be just as comfortable and well furnished as the ones indoors.

Rugs are an important part of that notion, whether they're used to soften a cedar deck or to simply add color to a con-crete patio. Bamboo rugs are an increasingly popular option, not only because they're durable, but also because they come in so many fashionable colors and patterns. Plus, bamboo is a sustainable material, as is hemp. While rugs made of hemp may not be as readily available as those made of bamboo, they are similar in strength and resilience.

Bamboo

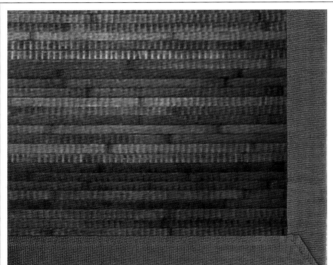

- Bamboo, a sustainable fiber, is strong enough to be used for rugs indoors or out.

- A variety of silk-screened designs are available, with something to suit everyone's styles and tastes, and these easy-to-clean rugs are mold-, mildew-, and water-resistant.

- Some rugs have synthetic backings to give them extra cushioning and make them nonslip.

- Bamboo rugs used on protected porches or patios will last longer than those left completely out in the elements.

Hemp

- Rugs made of 100 percent hemp are durable enough to be used outdoors.

- Hemp rugs are available in a wide variety of colors and styles.

- Although these rugs are not machine washable, they can be cleaned with a mild detergent and small brush and then rinsed thoroughly.

- One of the most eco-friendly natural resources, hemp grows quickly without the use of pesticides or chemicals.

One of the most basic types of floor coverings, rush mats have versatility going for them, too. Well suited for a porch or patio that has some degree of protection, rush mats fold or roll up easily and can go with you to yoga practice or your next picnic. As for recycled options, you can breathe a little easier knowing that many plastic soda bottles are escaping landfills and being used to make reversible outdoor rugs. Even old flip-flops are being transformed into colorful rugs with outdoor durability.

MAKE IT EASY

With just a little imagination and elbow grease, you can add a permanent "rug" to a concrete patio. Draw the pattern of your choice onto the concrete floor, then use paints or stains (specifically formulated to be used on this type of surface and, preferably, eco-friendly) to complete your custom creation.

Rush Mats

- Rush mats are made of the stalks or hollow stemlike leaves of a variety of plants.

- Mats made of natural rush, an aquatic plant, are durable and extremely versatile.

- This natural plant material is characterized by a light neutral hue that complements any setting.

- Lightweight and easy to roll up, rush mats can be used for floor coverings as well as outdoor play mats for children.

Recycled

- Made entirely from recycled plastic soda bottles, rugs made of polypropylene strands work well outdoors.

- Colorful patterns are woven in a way to make the rugs reversible; one side is just as attractive as the other.

- This type of rug also works well in mudrooms and kitchens, wherever there's daily wear and tear.

- To clean this kind of recycled rug, simply wash it down with a hose.

OUTDOOR LIVING

FINISHING TOUCHES

Little details in an outdoor setting can make a big impact on the environment.

Inside your home, it's the finishing touches that add an element of personality. It's no different, either, when it comes to outdoor living. The right accents will not only provide a clue to your personal style preferences, but also give your guests insight to the importance you place on the environment.

Some choices are more obvious in their green approach than others. Nary will a guest know, for instance, that the fire bowl they're gathered around is made of recycled cast iron. The same goes for the nearby hammock, for that matter. It may look just like the conventional cotton variety, even if it's crafted from recycled soda bottles. The two different hammocks may be similar in appearance, but the recycled version

Copper Fire Bowl

- As opposed to an outdoor fireplace that allows you to sit in front of it, a freestanding fire bowl allows guests to gather all around.

- A fire bowl has the advantage of being portable, so you can move it from place to place.

- Some freestanding fire bowls come with screened covers that add an element of safety.

- The heavy metal used to make the bowl keeps it securely in the stand.

Recycled Hammock

- Whether hung from a stand or suspended between two trees, hammocks are soothing to both mind and body.

- Traditionally made of all-cotton rope, hammocks are now being crafted from recycled materials.

- This hammock's constructed from recycled soda bottles, creating a fiber that's as comfortable as cotton but impervious to water.

- The white-oak stretcher bars are finished with natural linseed oil.

goes a long way toward keeping plastic out of local landfills.

Guests are sure to take notice of a cork birdhouse, though—if they see it, that is. Its very material camouflages it well against the bark of a tree. There's no chance, however, that they'll miss the sight or sound of a soothing water fountain. But they'll surely be impressed that it's made of bamboo, and even more when they find out it runs on nothing more than solar power.

································· GREEN ● LIGHT ·····················

Making a green effort doesn't have to be expensive. Add a splash of color to your outdoor table, for instance, with coasters made of recycled materials. You'll find them made of circuit board, metal traffic signs, even old record albums. Not only will they protect your table; they're sure to be conversation starters, too.

Cork Birdhouse

- Eco-friendly concepts can apply to birdhouses just like they do to human homes.

- This lightweight birdhouse, designed specifically for small birds, is made from nonendangered cork.

- Because the birdhouse is designed with no perch, larger predatory birds can't land and/or take up residence.

- Its camouflage aspect is attractive to feathered friends, too; the birdhouse blends right in with the bark of a tree.

Bamboo Fountain

- A water fountain that operates on solar energy, like this one does, is more eco-friendly than one that requires electricity.

- Known in Japan as a "deer chaser," this fountain combines the soothing sound of falling water with a soft, tapping rhythm.

- Made of solid bamboo, the fountain is mounted to a rot-resistant base.

- Just twenty inches high, this fountain melds easily into any landscape.

OUTDOOR LIVING

FRAMEWORK

Eco-friendly tactics are increasingly common when it comes to home construction.

If you're about to embark on the building process, why not make your place green from the ground up? Some tried-and-true construction techniques have long been eco-friendly, while others are on the cutting-edge of green technology.

Steel, for instance, has been used as a framing material for decades. Appropriate for projects large and small, steel is practically indestructible and fire resistant, too. Meanwhile, thanks to the green movement, another framing technique—straw-bale construction—is seeing a revival. Once a post-and-beam frame is completed, the straw bales can go up, creating walls that ultimately get sealed with stucco or plaster. The result is a well-insulated house with the look of

Steel

- Strong and lightweight at the same time, steel has historically been a preferred material for construction, primarily for framing purposes.

- Ore, coal, and limestone are the primary components of steel.

- Steel can be used for everything from single-family houses to multi-unit apartments to commercial buildings.

- Some of steel's best attributes are that it's resistant to fire and insect damage, and it stands up well to extreme weather conditions.

Straw Bales

- Straw-bale construction takes advantage of a very sustainable resource.

- New construction is usually done in a non-loadbearing style, with the bales making up the walls within a supportive post-and-beam frame.

- This kind of construction is cost-efficient, providing good insulation and sound proofing.

- The bales must be kept dry throughout the building process or they will start to deteriorate, which can eventually cause structural problems.

a Southwest-style adobe home that's cost-efficient to build and to heat, as well.

Even the lumber used today has an eco-friendly twist. Look for wood that has the Forest Stewardship Council (FSC) seal, which certifies that it has come from forests managed in an environmentally and socially responsible way. Hardwoods, softwoods, veneers, and even particle-board can have the FSC seal. That includes many of today's engineered woods, too. The thin veneer top layer, as well as the substrate, is just as likely to be produced in a responsible way.

Certified Wood

- The FSC certifies hardwood and softwood lumber, hardwood veneer, and particleboard.

- An FSC certification guarantees that wood comes from forests managed in an environmentally and socially responsible way.

- Before being certified, a forest must be evaluated based on management practices in three areas: sustainable harvest, ecosystem health, and community benefits.

- Many retailers stock FSC-certified products.

Engineered Wood

- Engineered wood has the same kind of strength and beauty as hardwoods, but a fraction of the weight.

- This type of wood consists of a thin layer of wood veneer glued on top of a layer of plywood.

- The surface of engineered wood is smoother and more level than its hardwood counterparts.

- Engineered woods are generally less affected by moisture than hardwoods.

BUILDING BLOCKS

DOORS

Whether you're looking for a new door or a stylish old one, be sure that it's eco-friendly.

Doors are more than mere passageways. They're insulators, safeguards, and provide an opportunity to make an eco-friendly decorative statement.

Some homeowners won't consider anything but a solid-wood door. And why would they? Wood has a warm, inherent beauty that's hard to beat. Truly green doors, however, are made of wood that's been certified by the FSC. FSC-certified products are readily available in most home centers. All it takes is a little background check of the products your retailer carries; specifically, ask about the product's Chain of Custody certificate.

Not surprisingly, bamboo is also showing up in doors. This

FSC-Certified Doors

- A door that's truly green utilizes renewable and sustainably harvested materials for its components.

- Look for wood doors that have been certified by the FSC at specialty retailers and major home improvement stores.

- Wood products that have the FSC seal can be tracked from the finished item all the way back to the certified forest of origin, giving them Chain of Custody certification.

Bamboo

- Structurally sound and aesthetically appealing, bamboo is a good choice for doors.

- Bamboo is extremely sustainable. The day after a stalk is harvested, there can be four to seven plants growing in its place.

- There's a wide variety of styles available in solid or hollow-core doors, ranging from traditional to ultra-contemporary.

- Bamboo doors can either be natural (light) or carbonized (dark) and designed with or without glass.

sustainable and most durable product can have a light, natural finish or take on a dark, carbonized hue. Because bamboo is also appropriate for flooring, it's easy to find a door similar in color to that of your floor. Meanwhile, wheat board is another material getting high marks for its sustainability. Utilizing straw waste material to form its core, this door is tremendously stable and moderately priced, too.

There are many possibilities presented by used doors—and those made of reclaimed wood. You could end up with a one-of-a-kind model that's the envy of the neighborhood.

Wheat Board

- Wheat-board doors, one of the most sustainable types, are constructed using straw waste products.

- A stable wheat-board core eliminates the possibility of any warping, cracking, or splitting, which means that the door will last longer.

- Low-VOC (volatile organic compound) adhesives are used throughout the construction process of this door type.

- Wheat-board doors, available in a wide variety of sizes and styles, can be either painted or stained.

Reclaimed Wood

- Another sustainable route is to look for used doors or those made of reclaimed wood.

- By using a salvaged door, you eliminate the loss of energy associated with building a new door.

- Reclaimed wood—from oak and elm to walnut and fir—can be used to create custom doors.

- Both used doors and those made of reclaimed wood have a patina that can only develop over time.

BUILDING BLOCKS

WINDOWS

By choosing green windows you can save energy—and money in the long run, too.

On one hand they let in natural light and, on the other, they allow energy to escape. But the right window will help you save energy and maximize natural light. And once you choose the right windows for you, positioning is paramount; by maximizing daylight, you can reduce your heating needs.

Strongly consider windows specifically labeled as energy efficient. It makes sense that double-pane windows are twice as efficient as single-pane versions, but think twice about opting for triple- or quadruple-pane varieties. While they certainly increase the savings, they multiply the weight, too. Instead, look for windows—including those that are Energy Star certified—that will give you the same benefits at less

Energy Efficient

- Because a large percentage of your home's energy can be lost through the windows, use energy-efficient types.

- State-of-the-art glazing systems can protect a home's interior from harmful UV rays while letting in more natural light.

- Energy-efficient windows reduce condensation as well as overall heating and cooling costs.

- Some companies have their own specific energy-efficient designations, while others are generally Energy Star certified.

Skylights

- Skylights installed on the roof bring in light from the sun's most direct angle.

- Some raised models collect the light above the roof level. Then they transfer the light through a mirror-finish aluminum pipe that directs the light to a diffusing lens in the ceiling.

- At high noon, a 13-inch version of this type of skylight can deliver more sunlight than a dozen 100-watt light bulbs.

- This type of skylight can often be installed by a homeowner in just a few hours.

218

cost. While you're at it, take a look at skylights, too, which give your home access to the sun from the most direct angle.

As for the window frames, wood has traditionally been a good choice, and it remains so—especially frames made of FSC-certified species. By doing a little homework, you'll discover they're more readily available than you might think. But if you're building a new house with vintage style, don't overlook custom windows crafted with reclaimed wood. They have character and an aged patina that's hard to beat.

Wood Window Frames

- Window frames made of wood have a green advantage, because they don't have to be replaced very often.

- Wood window frames are typically crafted in classic architecture styles and fitted with energy-efficient panes.

- It's not unusual for wood window frames to have hand-cast hardware, lending to the look of authenticity.

- Wood window frames need to be repainted or restained every few years but seldom replaced.

Recycled Windows

- Window frames made of reclaimed wood can be custom-crafted to any shape or size.

- Reclaimed wood window frames are a good fit for new projects that have a vintage look.

- Reclaimed wood window frames can be fitted with energy-efficient glass, which gives them a green boost.

- Good sources for vintage windows—ready to be recycled—are antiques stores and salvage shops.

BUILDING BLOCKS

219

DECKING

New, reclaimed, and recycled decking can all be good green choices.

There's nothing like retreating to the deck for a little rest and relaxation. And today's decks are more elaborate than ever, easily accommodating large groups of family and friends. The downside is that these oversize spaces require more materials. That's why it's more important than ever to make careful choices when building the deck of your dreams.

If your plan is to build a hardwood deck, look for species that support the green effort. FSC-certified lumber is readily available, even in your local home improvement store. On the other hand, if you want something more exotic, consider tropical hardwoods. Species such as Ipe and Tigrewood are sustainably harvested, which you can verify through a Chain

Hardwood

- Because they are harder than redwood, cedar, or pine, tropical hardwoods—such as Ipe and Tigrewood—are often used for decking.

- These woods are sustainably harvested, which can be verified through a Chain of Custody certificate.

- Tropical hardwoods resist splitting and splintering.

- These types of wood can be sealed to preserve their original color or left to weather to a soft gray.

Reclaimed Wood

- Redwood is often reclaimed and used for home improvement projects such as decks and patios.

- Redwood is prized for its beauty, its resistance to decay, and its ability to stand up to the elements.

- When oiled, redwood retains a rosy hue, but, when left unfinished, it weathers to a silver gray.

- Teak is another type of reclaimed wood often used for decking purposes.

of Custody certificate. A "chain of custody" can apply to many things, documenting the history and/or ownership of something—from legal evidence to medical test results. From a green point of view, however, it refers to tracking the custodianship of wood and wood products along the supply chain from harvest to distribution of the final product.

A deck's casual attitude makes reclaimed wood a good option, too. Redwood and teak are two species you'll most easily find, both of which weather to a soft, silver gray. Cedar decking, a perennially popular choice, naturally weathers in

much the same way, but you can also finish it in your choice of stains.

Beyond the obvious environmental advantage, composite (recycled) decking doesn't warp or splinter, not only enhancing its appearance but also making it easier on bare feet. Made of combined recycled plastic grocery bags, reclaimed pallet wrap, and waste wood, it can even be given a textured wood grain. The larger your deck, the more you'll be doing for the environment, too.

Composite Wood

- Composite decking is typically made with a combination of recycled plastic grocery bags, reclaimed pallet wrap, and waste wood.

- The plastic element shields the decking from moisture and insect damage, so there is no rotting or splintering.

- This product has excellent traction, even when wet.

- The wood in this decking provides protection from UV damage.

- This material sometimes has subtle woodgrain-like variations and/or an embossed wood texture.

Cedar

- Decking made of red cedar has a rich color and an unmistakable fragrance—one of its most admired qualities.

- Red cedar is naturally resistant to the rain and sun and, specifically, potentially harmful UV rays.

- This type of decking material is also naturally resistant to insect damage.

- Cedar can be stained or allowed to naturally weather to a soft silver-gray hue.

FOR A RAINY DAY

Conserving water is one of the best steps you can take toward going green.

Because water is one of our most precious resources, it's more important than ever to conserve as much as possible. But you can work in tandem with Mother Nature toward achieving this goal. By catching and reusing rain water, you'll take a giant step toward going green.

Rain chains, for instance, can be attached to gutters in a matter of minutes, serving the same purpose as conventional downspouts. Both simple link styles and chains with decorative cups guide the rain gently downward—right into a catchment barrel, if you like. If you're truly serious about water conservation, however, choose rain chains that are more functional and less decorative. Another way to collect large

Rain Chains

- Rain chains offer a decorative alternative to traditional closed-metal or plastic downspouts.

- This type of chain breaks the fall of the water, guiding it downward to the ground, into a basin, or into a catchment barrel.

- Rain chains are typically made of copper, brass, aluminum, and iron.

- The rain cups along this chain have open bottoms to allow for an efficient water flow, even during heavy rainfall.

Rain Tubes

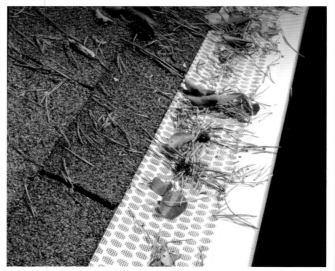

- Rain tubes eliminate clogged downspouts that result in overflowing gutters.

- Placed inside the gutters themselves, these tubes capture water as quickly as an open gutter but keep out leaves and large debris.

- The tubes are made from 100 percent postconsumer recycled materials.

- Although these tubes have a long life span, they can still be recycled over and over again.

amounts of rain water is with rain tubes; they prevent downspouts from clogging, even through heavy debris. Made of 100 percent recycled materials, rain tubes fit snugly into the gutters themselves, keeping debris out of way of the water stream so as much as possible goes straight to the catchment barrel. Similarly, some gutter guards, sometimes called rain heads, feature multiple screens to deflect leaves and debris away from the flow of water. At the same time, they improve the quality of the water going into the catchment barrel and reduce maintenance on the catchment barrel, too.

As for the barrel itself, look for one that is topped with an aluminum mesh screen, providing yet another filter for the water that you collect. It will keep out free-falling leaves, stray pieces of shingles, sticks, and other debris that falls off the roof. Be sure, however, that the screen is easily removable for cleaning and storage. An overflow attachment is a good idea, too. An efficient one will draw excess water down and away from the barrel, diverting it away from your home's foundation.

Gutter Guards

Water Catchment

- A conventional guard keeps gutters from becoming blocked, but this unit also improves water quality.

- By screening leaves onto the ground, it prevents gutters from blocking and eliminates a fire hazard.

- A secondary stainless steel screen is included to keep mosquitoes and vermin out of downpipes in a "wet" system.

- With the removal of the secondary screen, this gutter guard can remove debris even when rainwater is not being collected.

- Molded of thick, recycled plastic, this 54-gallon barrel will catch water from a rain chain or downspout for later use in your home or garden.

- The system includes a removable aluminum top screen to keep out debris, as well as a handy spigot.

- An overflow tube keeps excess water away from the foundation of your house.

- Because it's flat on one side, this barrel can fit snugly against an exterior wall.

BUILDING BLOCKS

225

RESOURCES

There's a virtual wealth of green resources available today. To help you in your search, look to the following Web sites. Some include green products as a part of their overall inventory, while others are dedicated to green items only. Keep in mind that many of the sites listed offer more than one type of product. If you find a site you like in the furniture category, for instance, browse around and you may also find nursery items as well as finishing touches for your home, too.

Shades of Green

Aurora Glass www.auroraglass.org
Branch www.branchhome.com
Coyuchi www.coyuchiorganic.com
Eco-artware www.eco-artware.com
EcoSofa, part of EcoChoices www.ecosofa.com
FLOR www.flor.com
Gaiam www.gaiam.com
Green Earth Office Supply greenearthofficesupply.stores.yahoo.net
Kohler www.kohler.com
Smith & Fong Plyboo www.plyboo.com
Terramai www.terramai.com

Furniture

Acronym Designs www.acronymdesigns.com
A Natural Home www.anaturalhome.com
Bamboo Hardwoods www.bamboohardwoods.com
BDDW www.bddw.com
Bean Products www.beanproducts.com
Branch www.branchhome.com
Breathe Easy www.breatheeasycabinetry.com
Cambium Studio www.cambiumstudio.com
David Colwell www.davidcolwell.com

Design Within Reach www.dwr.com
Ecohaus www.environmentalhomecenter.com
Environment Furniture www.environment-furniture.com
Eric Manigian www.ericmanigian.com
Furnature www.furnature.com
GREENCulture www.eco-furniture.com
Greener Lifestyles www.greenerlifestyles.com
Iannone www.i-sdesign.com
IF Green www.ifgreen.com
La-Z-Boy, Todd Oldham Collection www.lazboy.com/oldham
Lee Industries www.leeindustries.com
MetaForm Studio www.metaformstudio.com
Natural Tree Furniture www.naturaltreefurniture.com
Neil Kelly Cabinets www.neilkellycabinets.com
Niche www.design-niche.com
Pacific Rim Woodworking www.pacificrimwoodworking.com
Sachi Organics www.sachiorganics.com
Scrapile www.scrapile.com
Tamalpais www.tamalpais.com
Teak Collection www.quality-teak.com
The Period House www.theperiodhouse.com
Uhuru www.uhurudesign.com
Verde Design Studio www.verdedesignstudio.net
Viesso www.viesso.com
VivaTerra www.vivaterra.com
Vivavi www.vivavi.com
Whit McLeod www.whitmcleod.com

Fabrics

Ambatalia Fabrics www.ambataliafabrics.com
Angela Adams www.angelaadams.com
Branch www.branchhome.com
Country Curtains www.countrycurtains.com
EnviroTextiles www.envirotextile.com

Gaiam www.gaiam.com
GreenSage www.greensage.com
Indika Organics www.indikaorganics.com
Libeco Home www.libecohomestores.com
Madeline Weinrib www.madelineweinrib.com
Mod Green Pod www.modgreenpod.com
Natural Lee www.naturallee.com
NearSea Naturals www.nearseanaturals.com
Pottery Barn www.potterybarn.com
Rawganique www.rawganique.com
Smith & Noble www.smithandnoble.com
The Silk Trading Co. www.silktrading.com
VivaTerra www.vivaterra.com
Vivavi www.vivavi.com

Paints and Finishes

AFM Safecoat www.afmsafecoat.com
Aglaia Paint www.aglaiapaint.com
American Pride Paint www.americanpridepaint.com
Anna Sova www.annasova.com
Auro www.aurousa.com
Benjamin Moore www.benjaminmoore.com
BioShield www.bioshieldpaint.com
Duron www.duron.com
Ecohaus www.environmentalhomecenter.com
Eco-Products www.ecoproducts.com
Green Planet Paints www.greenplanetpaints.com
Green Sacramento www.greensacramento.com
Kelly-Moore Paints www.kellymoore.com
Miller Paint Co. www.millerpaint.com
Mythic www.mythicpaint.com
Natural Home Design Center
www.naturalhomeproducts.com
Olympic www.olympic.com
Sherwin-Williams www.sherwin-williams.com
Silent Paint Remover www.silentpaintremover.com
SoyClean www.soyclean.biz

The Earth Pigments Company www.earthpigments.com
The Old Fashioned Milk Paint Co. www.milkpaint.com
This Old Grout & Stone www.thisoldgrout.com
The Period House www.theperiodhouse.com
Tile Shack www.tileshack.com
Tried and True Wood Finishes
www.triedandtruewoodfinish.com
Yolo Colorhouse www.yolocolorhouse.com

Wall Coverings

American Clay www.americanclay.com
Branch www.branchhome.com
Build Direct www.builddirect.com
Coverings Etc www.coveringsetc.com
Eco Friendly Flooring www.ecofriendlyflooring.com
Fireclay Tile www.fireclaytile.com
Kirei www.kireiusa.com
Mannington www.mannington.com
Modwalls www.modwalls.com
Oceanside Glasstile www.glasstile.com
Phillip Jeffries Ltd. www.phillipjeffries.com
Sandhill Industries www.sandhillind.com
Seattle Architectural Finishing Studio www.seattleafs.com
Smith & Fong Plyboo www.plyboo.com
Stone Source www.stonesource.com
Terramai www.terramai.com

Window Coverings

Carolina Window Blinds www.carolinawindowblinds.com
Earth Care www.earthcarewindows.com
Earthshade www.earthshade.com
Gaiam www.gaiam.com
Hunter Douglas www.hunterdouglas.com
IFA www.ifablinds.com
Insolroll www.insolroll.com
Legacy Window Coverings www.legacywindowcoverings.com
MechoShade www.mechoshade.com
North Solar Screen www.northsolarscreen.com

Smith & Noble www.smithandnoble.com
The Bamboo Site www.thebamboosite.com
Window Film Depot www.windowfilmdepot.com

Soft Floor Coverings

Angela Adams www.angelaadams.com
Earth Weave Carpet Mills www.earthweave.com
Eco-artware www.eco-artware.com
Ecohaus www.environmentalhomecenter.com
Eco-Products www.ecoproducts.com
Elizabeth Eakins www.elizabetheakins.com
Emma Gardner Design www.emmagardnerdesign.com
Fibreworks www.fibreworks.com
Gaiam www.gaiam.com
Green Floors www.greenfloors.com
Kushtush Organics www.kushtush.com
Madeline Weinrib www.madelineweinrib.com
Merida www.meridameridian.com
Natural Area Rugs www.naturalarearugs.com
Natural Elements www.natural-elements.net
Sisal Rugs Direct www.sisalrugs.com
The Natural Carpet Company www.naturalcarpetcompany.com
VivaTerra www.vivaterra.com

Hard Floor Coverings

Aronson's Floor Covering www.aronsonsfloors.com
Bamboo Mountain www.bamboomountain.com
Bettencourt www.bettencourtwood.com
Eco-Products www.ecoproducts.com
Enviroglas www.enviroglasproducts.com
Expanko www.expanko.com
Fast Floors www.fastfloors.com
FGS PermaShine www.fgs-permashine.com
Forbo www.themarmoleumstore.com
Goodwin Heart Pine www.heartpine.com
Globus Cork www.corkfloor.com

Green Floors www.greenfloors.com
Linoleum Store www.linoleumstore.com
Nova www.novafloorings.com
Scofield www.scofield.com
Smith & Fong Plyboo www.plyboo.com
Stained Concrete www.stainedconcrete.org
The Bamboo Site www.thebamboosite.com

Planks and Tiles

Ann Sacks www.annsacks.com
Arrow Tile www.arrowtiles.com
BarroNica www.barronica.com
Bedrock Industries www.bedrockindustries.com
Brick Floor Tile, Inc. www.brick-floor-tile.com
Build Direct www.builddirect.com
Country Floors www.countryfloors.com
Crossville www.crossvilleinc.com
Eco Friendly Flooring www.ecofriendlyflooring.com
Ecohaus www.environmentalhomecenter.com
Eleek www.eleekinc.com
FLOR www.flor.com
Globus Cork www.corkfloor.com
Green Building Supply www.greenbuildingsupply.com
Green Floors www.greenfloors.com
Green Mountain Soapstone www.greenmountainsoapstone.com
Green Sacramento www.greensacramento.com
Hakatai www.hakatai.com
Happy Floors www.happy-floors.com
Imagine Tile www.imaginetile.com
MarbleMaster www.marblemaster.com
Oceanside Glasstile www.glasstile.com
Old Grain www.oldgrain.com
Quarry Tile Company www.quarrytile.com
Terra Green www.terragreenceramics.com
The Bamboo Site www.thebamboosite.com

Countertops

ACE www.aceconcrete.com
Bettencourt www.bettencourtwood.com
Ceramic Design www.ceramicdesignltd.com
Circle City Copperworks www.circlecitycopperworks.com
Coverings Etc www.coveringsetc.com
Durat www.durat.com
Ecohaus www.environmentalhomecenter.com
Eleek www.eleekinc.com
Enviroglas www.enviroglasproducts.com
Fireclay Tile www.fireclaytile.com
Green Sacramento www.greensacramento.com
IceStone www.icestone.biz
MarbleMaster www.marblemaster.com
Oceanside Glasstile www.glasstile.com
Old World Butcher Block Furniture
www.butcherblockspecialist.com
Renewed Materials www.renewedmaterials.com
Richlite www.richlite.com
Soupcan www.soupcan.com
Specialty Stainless www.specialtystainless.com
Stone Forest www.stoneforest.com
Syndecrete www.syndecrete.com
Totally Bamboo www.totallybamboo.com
VitraStone www.vitrastone.com

Appliances

Amana www.amana.com
Bosch www.boschappliances.com
Fisher & Paykel www.fisherpaykel.com
Frigidaire www.frigidaire.com
GE www.geappliances.com
Kenmore www.kenmore.com
Kitchenaid www.kitchenaid.com
LGE us.lge.com
Maytag www.maytag.com
MicroFridge www.microfridge.com

Pūr www.purwaterfilter.com
Sub-Zero www.subzero.com
Sun Frost www.sunfrost.com
TerraFlo www.terraflo.com
Viking www.vikingrange.com

Bed and Bath

Allergy Buyers Club www.allergybuyersclubshopping.com
Amenity Home www.amenityhome.com
Anna Sova www.annasova.com
Building for Health www.buildingforhealth.com
Caroma www.caromausa.com
Coverest www.coverest.com
Coyuchi www.coyuchiorganic.com
Cuddledown www.cuddledown.com
Delta Faucet www.deltafaucet.com
Durat www.durat.com
EcoBathroom www.ecobathroom.com
EcoBedroom www.ecobedroom.com
Eleek www.eleekinc.com
Good Night Naturals www.goodnightnaturals.com
Green Sleep www.greensleep.com
Haiku Designs www.haikudesigns.com
Heart of Vermont www.heartofvermont.com
Indika Organics www.indikaorganics.com
Lifekind www.lifekind.com
Loop looporganic.com
Natura www.naturaworld.com
Nirvana Safe Haven www.nontoxic.com
Organic Mattresses www.organicmattresses.com
Oxygenics www.oxygenics.com
Pottery Barn www.potterybarn.com
Pure-Rest Organics www.purerest.com
Ralph Lauren www.ralphlauren.com
Rawganique www.rawganique.com
Sachi Organics www.sachiorganics.com
Satara www.satara-inc.com

Shepherd's Dream www.shepherdsdream.com
Syndecrete www.syndecrete.com
Target www.target.com
The Clean Bedroom www.thecleanbedroom.com
The Company Store www.thecompanystore.com
The Organic Mattress Store www.theorganicmattressstore.com
VivaTerra www.vivaterra.com
Vivetique www.vivetique.com
West Elm www.westelm.com
White Lotus Home www.whitelotus.net

Plumbing Products

AM Conservation Group www.amconservationgroup.com
American Standard www.americanstandard-us.com
Cement Elegance www.cement-elegance.com
Crane Plumbing www.craneplumbing.com
Ecohaus www.environmentalhomecenter.com
EcoWater Systems www.ecowater.com
Eleek www.eleekinc.com
Eljer www.eljer.com
Filters Fast www.filtersfast.com
Fine Crafts & Imports www.finecraftsimports.com
Gaiam Living www.gaiam.com
Kohler www.kohler.com
Mrs. Meyers www.mrsmeyers.com
Oxygenics www.oxygenics.com
Planet www.planetinc.com
Seventh Generation www.seventhgen.com
Sinks Gallery www.sinksgallery.com
Stone Forest www.stoneforest.com
Stone Soup Concrete www.stonesoupconcrete.com
Vintage Tub & Bath www.vintagetub.com

Nursery

Allergy Buyers Club www.allergybuyersclubshopping.com
Amenity Home www.amenityhome.com
A Natural Home www.anaturalhome.com

Argington www.argington.com
Baby Bunz & Co. www.babybunz.com
Babyworks www.babyworks.com
BioShield www.bioshieldpaint.com
Burt's Bees www.burtsbees.com
California Baby www.californiababy.com
Celery www.celeryfurniture.com
Cotton Monkey www.cottonmonkey.com
Coyuchi www.coyuchiorganic.com
Crystal Baby Organics www.crystalbabyorganics.com
Ducduc www.ducducnyc.com
Ecobaby www.ecobaby.com
EcoBedroom www.ecobedroom.com
EcoTimber www.ecotimber.com
FLOR www.flor.com
Gary Weeks and Company www.garyweeks.com
Iglooplay www.iglooplay.com
Kushtush Organics www.kushtush.com
Lifekind www.lifekind.com
Lilipad Studio lilipadstudio.com
Little Merry Fellows www.littlemerryfellows.com
Modern Tots www.moderntots.com
Naturepedic www.naturepedic.com
Nui Organics www.nuiorganics.com
Nurseryworks www.nurseryworks.net
Q Junior www.qcollectionjunior.com
Sachi Organics www.sachiorganics.com
Sage Baby www.sagebabynyc.com
Sage Creek www.sagecreeknaturals.com
Satara www.satara-inc.com
Smith & Noble www.smithandnoble.com
The Clean Bedroom www.thecleanbedroom.com
The Land of Nod www.landofnod.com
The Old Fashioned Milk Paint Co. www.milkpaint.com
Vivavi www.vivavi.com

Lighting

A.R.E. Naturals www.arenaturals.com
Best Home LED Lighting www.besthomeledlighting.com
Destination Lighting www.destinationlighting.com
Electrical Supplies Online www.electricsuppliesonline.com
Eleek www.eleekinc.com
Energy Supermarket shop.solardirect.com
Gaiam Living www.gaiam.com
Green Home www.greenhome.com
Koncept www.koncepttech.com
Natural Collection www.naturalcollection.com
Perch! Design www.perchdesign.net
Re:Modern www.re-modern.com
Rogan Objects www.roganobjects.com
Shine www.shineeveryday.com
VivaTerra www.vivaterra.com
Y Lighting www.ylighting.com

Finishing Touch

Acacia www.acaciacatalog.com
Balanced Design www.balanced-design.com
Bamboo Hardwoods www.bamboohardwoods.com
Bambu www.bambuhome.com
Branch www.branchhome.com
Chiasso www.chiasso.com
Cobre www.ecobre.com
Eco-artware www.eco-artware.com
Fire & Light www.fireandlight.com
Gaiam Living www.gaiam.com
GoodHumans www.goodhumans.com
GREENCulture www.eco-furniture.com
Natural Spaces www.naturalspaces.com
Organic Bouquet www.organicbouquet.com
Perch! Design www.perchdesign.net
Recycled Glassworks www.recycledglassworks.com
Resource Revival www.resourcerevival.com
Shademiami www.shademiami.com

Spectra Décor www.spectradecor.com
The Green Glass Co. www.greenglass.com
The Land of Nod www.landofnod.com
Trillium Artisans www.trilliumartisans.org
VivaTerra www.vivaterra.com

Pets

8 in 1 www.eightinonepet.com
A Natural Home anaturalhome.com
Annie's Sweatshop www.anniessweatshop.com
Bailey and Wags www.baileyandwags.com
Belladog www.belladog.com
Botanical Dog www.botanicaldog.com
Branch www.branchhome.com
CatCouture www.catcouture.com
Cats Rule|Dogs Rock www.catsrule.com
Cuddledown www.cuddledown.com
Earth Animal www.earthanimal.com
Earth Dog www.earthdog.com
Earth Doggy www.earthdoggy.com
Earth Friendly Products www.ecos.com
EcoAnimal www.ecoanimal.com
Feline Pine www.catsrule.com
Furlong's Pet Supply—Cuddledown www.cuddledown.com
George www.georgesf.com
Great Green Pet www.greatgreenpet.com
Green Dog Pet Supply www.greendogpetsupply.com
Holden Designs www.holdendesigns.com
Natural Pet Market www.naturalpetmarket.com
Official Dog House www.officialdoghouse.com
Only Natural Pet Store www.onlynaturalpet.com
Palmetto Pet Gear www.palmettopet.com
PetGuard www.petguard.com
PetSage www.petsage.com
Planet Dog www.planetdog.com
Robbins Pet Care www.robbinspetcare.com

Simply Fido www.simplyfido.com
Thayer & Ridge www.thayerandridge.com
The Pet Store Online www.thepetstoreonline.com
Vivavi www.vivavi.com
West Paw Design www.westpawdesign.com

Outdoor Living

American Recycled Plastic www.itsrecycled.com
A Natural Home www.anaturalhome.com
Bamboo Hardwoods www.bamboohardwoods.com
Destination Lighting www.destinationlighting.com
Gaiam Living www.gaiam.com
GREENCulture www.eco-furniture.com
Hobble Creek Trading Co. www.1cabinfurniture.com
Kayu Kayu www.kayukayu.com
Loll Designs www.lolldesigns.com
Natural Area Rugs www.naturalarearugs.com
Perch! Design www.perchdesign.net
Spirit Elements www.spiritelements.com
Urban Garden Center www.urbangardencenter.com

Building Blocks

Bettencourt www.bettencourtwood.com
Bonded Logic www.bondedlogic.com
CertainTeed www.certainteed.com
ChoiceDek www.choicedek.com
Columbia Forest Products www.columbiaforestproducts.com
COORitalia www.cooritalia.com
Eco-Products www.ecoproducts.com
Enviro Friendly Products www.enviro-friendly.com
Four Seasons Sunrooms www.fourseasonssunrooms.com
Goodwin Heart Pine www.heartpine.com
Green Building Supply www.greenbuildingsupply.com
Humabuilt www.humabuilt.com
Loewen www.loewen.com
Marblemaster www.marblemaster.com
Marvin www.marvin.com

Old Grain www.oldgrain.com
Rain Harvesting www.rainharvesting.com
RainTube www.raintube.com
Terramai www.terramai.com
Trex www.trex.com
Valley Lumber Sales www.cedarshakeandshingle.com
Weather Shield www.weathershield.com
Western Oregon Door www.oregondoor.com

E-tailers

2modern www.2modern.com
3r Living www.3rliving.com
Abundant Earth www.abundantearth.com
Acacia www.acaciacatalog.com
A Happy Planet www.ahappyplanet.com
All Things Green www.allthingsgreen.net
Amenity Home www.amenityhome.com
Anna Sova www.annasova.com
A.R.E. Naturals www.arenaturals.com
Bellacor www.bellacor.com
Bettencourt www.bettencourtwood.com
Blue House www.shopbluehouse.com
Branch www.branchhome.com
Design Public www.designpublic.com
Earthsake www.earthsake.com
Eco Design Resources www.ecodesignresources.com
Eco Terric www.eco-terric.com
Equita www.shopequita.com
Gaiam Living www.gaiam.com
Green and More www.greenandmore.com
Greener Grass Design www.greenergrassdesign.com
Greenfeet www.store.greenfeet.com
Green Fusion Design Center
www.greenfusiondesigncenter.com
Green Home www.greenhome.com
Greenline Paper Company www.greenlinepaper.com
Green Nest www.greennest.com

Healthy Home www.healthyhome.com
Hemp Sisters www.hemp-sisters.com
Herb Trader www.herbtrader.com
Inmod www.inmod.com
Living Green www1.livinggreen.com
Mama's Earth www.mamasearth.com
Mio www.mioculture.com
Natural Collection www.naturalcollection.com
Natural Spaces www.naturalspaces.com
Nirvana Safe Haven www.nontoxic.com
Organic Style www.organicstyle.com
Our Green House www.ourgreenhouse.com
Pottery Barn www.potterybarn.com
Reform School www.reformschoolrules.com
Re:Modern www.re-modern.com
Specialty Living www.specialtyliving.com
Sundance www.sundancecatalog.com
The Green Office www.thegreenoffice.com
The Green Robin www.thegreenrobin.com
Uncommon Goods www.uncommongoods.com
Velocity Art and Design www.velocityartanddesign.com
VivaTerra www.vivaterra.com
Vivavi www.vivavi.com
White Lotus Home www.whitelotus.net
Zola www.zolafurnishings.com

General Information

Building Green www.buildinggreen.com
Earth 911 www.earth911.org
Ecocycle www.ecocycle.com
Energy Star www.energystar.gov
Fair Trade Labelling Organizations www.fairtrade.net
Forest Stewardship Council www.fscus.org
Green Demolitions www.greendemolitions.com
GreenDimes www.greendimes.com
Green-e www.green-e.org
Green Home Building www.greenhomebuilding.com
Green Home Guide www.greenhomeguide.com
GreenSage www.greensage.com
Green Seal www.greenseal.org
Healthy House Institute www.healthyhouseinstitute.com
LEED www.usgbc.org
Low Impact Living www.lowimpactliving.com
Oikos www.oikos.com
PlanIt Greener www.planitgreener.com
Rainforest Alliance www.rainforest-alliance.org
Steel Recycling Institute www.recycle-steel.org
Sustainable Furniture Council
www.sustainablefurniturecouncil.com
The Great Green List www.greatgreenlist.com

RESOURCES

GLOSSARY

Biodegradeable:
Materials that are biodegradable have the ability to decompose back into the environment after exposure to the air, sun, or moisture. Solid biodegradable products work their way back into the soil (also known as composting) and liquid products biodegrade into water.

Carbon Footprint:
A person's carbon footprint is a measure of the effect his or her daily activities have on the environment in terms of the greenhouse gases he or she produces, measured in units of carbon dioxide. The smaller a person's footprint is, the better it is for the environment.

Chain of Custody:
This term refers to the custodianship of wood and wood products, tracking it from the initial harvest to the final distribution. A Chain of Custody certificate ensures that a particular product originated in a responsibly managed forest.

Compact Fluorescent Bulbs (CFL):
A CFL is an energy-efficient alternative for a standard incandescent bulb. Compared to an incandescent, a CFL can save as much as thirty dollars in energy costs over its lifetime; the initial cost is slightly more but it lasts longer.

Compost:
Ingredients that make up compost are generally either wet or dry. Wet, or "green," ingredients include fruit and vegetable peelings, coffee grounds, tea bags, and egg shells, while dry, or "brown," ingredients include tissue paper, newspaper, and paper egg cartons.

Cradle-to-Cradle:
Products that have cradle-to-cradle designation are made up of materials that can—after their initial use or lifetime—have another purpose, such as being recycled or composted.

Energy Star:
Manufacturers and retailers are allowed to put the Energy Star label on those appliances that either meet or exceed standards set by the U.S. Environmental Protection Agency (EPA) and the U.S. Department of Energy.

EnergyGuide:
The EnergyGuide label on a new appliance estimates the product's energy consumption as well as its operating cost, based on the national average cost of electricity.

Fair Trade:
In a fair trade system, workers receive living wages and employment opportunities for the goods they produce. International organizations help the workers market and sell goods, such as crafts and agricultural products, for which they receive a stable, minimum price. Goods can be certified as Fair Trade by groups such as the Fair Trade Labelling Organization (FLO).

Forest Stewardship Council:
The Forest Stewardship Council (FSC) is a nonprofit organization devoted to the responsible management of the world's forests. The FSC certifies wood and wood products according to standards that ensure forestry is practiced in an environmentally responsible, socially beneficial, and economically viable way.

Green-e Certified:
Green-e is widely regarded as the nation's leading independent renewable energy certification and verification program. The program's purpose is to expand the market for clean, renewable energy by advancing awareness of renewable-energy options.

Greenhouse Gas:
Greenhouse gases, produced as a result of human activities, trap solar radiation and, as a result, contribute to climate change as well as the destruction of the ozone layer.

Green Label:
The Carpet and Rug Institute (CRI) has put into place a Green Label program that identifies products with low-VOC emissions. It also recently launched Green Label Plus, an enhanced program for carpet and adhesives that sets the bar even higher to ensure that customers are purchasing the lowest-emitting products on the market.

Green Seal:
Green Seal is an independent, nonprofit organization dedicated to promoting environmentally responsible products and services. The third-party certification group utilizes a life-cycle approach; each evaluation includes a review of material extraction, the manufacturing process, and recycling or disposal methods.

Hemp:
One of the most environmentally friendly fibers, hemp requires no pesticides or fertilizers, and uses very little water. Hemp is a fast-growing plant, too, and can be used to make everything from paper to textiles.

Kapok:

Made from the seed fiber of the Cieba tree, kapok is soft and down-like; often used in pillows, it provides excellent comfort and support. Because the fiber is harvested from the tree's seedpods, the tree itself isn't harmed in the process.

LED:

An LED (light emitting diode) bulb uses approximately 90 percent less energy than a standard incandescent and can last up to sixty-thousand hours. Long reserved for purposes such as car brake lights, LEDs now have many household uses.

LEED:

The Leadership in Energy and Environmental Design (LEED) Green Building Rating System™ is the nationally accepted benchmark for the design, construction, and operation of green buildings. Buildings can be certified at four different levels—Certified, Silver, Gold, and Platinum.

Low-E Glass:

Glass rated as low-E has what's referred to as "low emissivity," due to a film or metallic coating that reflects the sun's rays and keeps out radiant heat. This type of coating can reflect between 40 and 70 percent of transmitted heat while still allowing natural light to come through the window.

National Organic Program:

The National Organic Program (NOP) is the federal regulatory agency under the umbrella of the USDA that governs the labeling of food as organic.

Natural Latex:

Made from the sap of the rubber tree, natural latex (or rubber) is biodegradable and typically has a life span of at least twenty years.

Off-Gassing:

Off-gassing is the release of gas into the air from products, like some paints, that were treated with chemicals during the manufacturing process.

Organic:

Organic refers to the way agricultural products are grown and processed. In order to be classified as organic, products must be grown, raised, or dyed without the use of synthetic chemicals, heavy metals, or GMOs (genetically modified organisms). Additionally, they must be biodegradable and free of toxins and irritants.

Postconsumer Waste:

Postconsumer waste is material that has served its original purpose as a consumer item and, thus, has been discarded.

Postindustrial Waste:

Postindustrial waste (also referred to as preconsumer waste) is produced during manufacturing; fabric remnants, for instance, are postindustrial waste in the production of clothing.

Reclaimed:

Reclaimed materials are those that have been used before and have been reused without any reprocessing. They can be adapted in some way—cut to a different size or refinished, for instance—but basically retain their original form.

Recycled:

Recycled materials are those that would otherwise be designated as waste, but have been remanufactured to create an entirely new product. A well-worn sweater, for instance, might be woven into a new rug.

Renewable:

A renewable resource is one that is capable of being replenished, either by reproducing itself or through another natural process. As a general rule, the process takes no more than a few decades.

Sustainable Forest Management Standard:

This forest management standard is dedicated to the long-term health of forest ecosystems. Sustainable forest management standards include the American Tree Farm System (ATFS), Canada Standards Association (CSA), Forest Stewardship Council (FSC), Maine Master Logger Certification, and the Sustainable Forestry Initiative (SFI).

Volatile Organic Compounds:

Volatile organic compounds (VOCs) are often found in paints, stains, glues, and similar materials. They affect internal air quality, giving off potentially harmful vapors.

PHOTO CREDITS

Chapter 1

p. XII (right): Courtesy of Eco Choices.com
p. 1 (left): Courtesy of Plyboo.com
p. 1 (right): © Andy Gregg / Bike Furniture Design
p. 2 (right): Courtesy of See Jane Work
p. 3 (left): Courtesy of Gaiam
p. 3 (right): Courtesy of TerraMai
p. 4 (left): Courtesy of Rev-a-Shelf
p. 4 (right): © Justin Horrocks/istockphoto
p. 5 (left): Courtesy of BranchHome.com
p. 5 (right): Courtesy of Eco-Artware.com
p. 6 (left): Courtesy of Coyuchi.com
p. 6 (right): Courtesy of Behr
p. 7 (left): Courtesy of Flor
p. 7 (right): Courtesy of Gaiam
p. 8 (right): Courtesy of Kohler
p. 9 (left): Courtesy of Aurora Glass Foundry
p. 10 (left): © Maria Jeffs/istockphoto
p. 10 (right): Courtesy of Bosch
p. 11 (left): Courtesy of Gaiam
p. 11 (right): © Hans F. Meier/istockphoto

Chapter 2

p. 12 (left): Courtesy of Cisco Brothers Corp.
p. 12 (right): Courtesy of Tamalpais NatureWorks
p. 13 (left): Courtesy of Eco-Furniture.com
p. 13 (right): Courtesy of BranchHome.com
p. 14 (left): Courtesy of David Colwell
p. 14 (right): Courtesy of VivaTerra
p. 15 (left): Courtesy of Vivavi
p. 15 (right): Courtesy of el: Environmental Language
p. 16 (left): Courtesy of LEE Industries
p. 16 (right): Courtesy of Cisco Brothers Corp.
p. 17 (left): Courtesy of Cisco Brothers Corp.
p. 18 (left): Courtesy of el: Environmental Language
p. 18 (right): Courtesy of Michael Iannone/ IANNONE DESIGN LTD
p. 19 (left): Courtesy of ModernLink
p. 19 (right): Courtesy of Art with Function, Designers: Holland Seydel & Eliav Nissan, Photo: Kevin Loudon & Savanna Driggers
p. 20 (left): Courtesy of VivaTerra
p 20 (right): Courtesy of Home Source International
p. 21 (left): Courtesy of Bean Products
p. 21 (right): © Steve Bromberg Photography 2008
p. 22 (left): © Greg Goodman/Vermont-Woods.com
p. 22 (right): Courtesy of Koch and Co. Inc.
p. 23 (left): Courtesy of Kohler Co.
p. 23 (right): Courtesy of Bamboo Hardwoods

Chapter 3

p. 24 (left): Courtesy of LEE Industries
p. 254 (right): Courtesy of BranchHome.com
p. 25 (left): © prphotos.com
p. 25 (right): Courtesy of Design Within Reach
p. 26 (left): Courtesy of LEE Industries
p. 26 (right): Courtesy of Libco Home Stores
p. 27 (left): Courtesy of Smith and Noble
p. 27 (right): Courtesy of Kevin O'Brien Studio
p. 28 (left): Courtesy of Robert Cramer/RC Green.org
p. 28 (right): Photo by Stephen Jessup for Nicky Thomson
p. 29 (left): © Jupiterimages Corporation
p. 29 (right): Courtesy of BranchHome.com
p. 30 (left): Courtesy of LEE Industries.com
p. 30 (right): Courtesy of DreamSacks, Inc.
p. 31 (left): Courtesy of Smith and Noble
p. 31 (right): Courtesy of Dreamsacks, Inc.
p. 32 (left): Courtesy of Greener Lifestyles
p. 32 (right): Courtesy of Rawganique
p. 33 (left): Courtesy of Rawganique
p. 33 (right): Courtesy of BranchHome.com
p. 34 (left): © Anna Adesanya
p. 34 (right): Courtesy of VivaTerra
p. 35 (left): Courtesy of Branch Home
p. 35 (right): Courtesy of Vivavi

Chapter 4

p. 36 (left): © Mearicon/shutterstock
p. 36 (right): Courtesy of AFM Safecoat
p. 37 (left): © iofoto/shutterstock
p. 38 (left): Courtesy of BioShield Clay Paints
p. 38 (right): © Chang/istockphoto
p. 39 (left): Courtesy of The Old Fashioned Milk Paint Co., Inc.
p. 39 (right): Courtesy of prshots.com, reproready.com/Linum from Sweden
p. 40 (left): © Vangelis/shutterstock
p. 40 (right): Courtesy of prshots.com, reproready.com/House of Fraser
p. 41 (left): Courtesy of prshots.com, reproready.com/Crowne Paints
p. 41 (right): © Naomi Hasegawa/ istockphoto
p. 42 (left): © Andrew Hill/istockphoto
p. 42 (right): Courtesy of Kohler Co.
p. 43 (left): Courtesy of prshots.com, repro ready.com/Harvey's Furniture Store
p. 43 (right): © Angie Chauvin/shutterstock
p. 44 (left): Courtesy of prshots.com, reproready.com/Barker & Stonehouse
p. 44 (right): Courtesy of prshots.com, reproready.com/Harvey's Furniture Store
p. 45 (left): Courtesy of prshots.com, reproready.com/Barker & Stonehouse
p. 45 (right): © Paul Hill/istockphoto
p. 46 (left): Courtesy of Ann Sacks
p. 46 (right): Courtesy of Diamond Tech
p. 47 (left): Courtesy of photos.com
p. 47 (right): © Jim Jurica/istockphoto

Chapter 5

p. 48 (left): Courtesy of Phillip Jeffries
p. 48 (right): Courtesy of Phillip Jeffries
p. 49 (left) Courtesy of Woodson & Rummerfield's House of Design, Inc.
p. 50 (left): Courtesy of Bamboo Hardwoods
p. 50 (right): © istockphoto
p. 51 (left): Courtesy of Kirei USA
p. 51 (right): Courtesy of TerraMai
p. 52 (left): Courtesy of Build Green TV

PHOTO CREDITS

p. 114 (left): Courtesy of Frigo Design/ Custom Stainless Steel Countertop/ www.frigodesign.com
p. 114 (right): Courtesy of Circle City Copperworks
p. 115 (left): © Alexander Zavadsky/ shutterstock
p. 115 (right): © Baloncici/shutterstock

Chapter 11
p. 116 (left): Courtesy of Sunfrost
p. 116 (right): Courtesy of Maytag
p. 117 (left): Courtesy of Micorfridge
p. 117 (right): Courteys of Subzero
p. 118 (left): Courtesy of Wolf Appliances
p. 118 (right): Courtesy of Viking
p. 119 (left): Courtesy of Frigidaire
p. 119 (right): Courtesy if GE Appliances
p. 120 (left): Courtesy of Fisher Paykel
p. 120 (right): Courtesy of Bosch
p. 121 (left): Courtesy of Kitchen Aid
p. 122 (left): Courtesy of LG Home Appliances
p. 122 (right): Courtesy of LG Home Appliances
p. 123 (left): Courtesy of Bosch
p. 123 (right): Courtesy of Fisher Paykel
p. 124 (left): Courtesy of Amana
p. 124 (right): Courtesy of Frigidaire
p. 125 (left): Courtesy of LG Home Appliances
p. 125 (right): Courtesy of GE Appliances
p. 126 (left): Courtesy of Air-Purifiers-America.com
p. 126 (right): Courtesy of Air-Purifiers-America.com
p. 127 (left): © Muriel Lasure/shutterstock
p. 127 (right): Courtesy of New Wave Enviro Products, Inc

Chapter 12
p. 128 (left): Courtesy of Coyuchi
p. 128 (right): Courtesy of VivaTerra
p. 129 (left): © bluestocking/istockphoto
p. 129 (right): Courtesy of VivaTerra
p. 130 (left): © shutterstock
p. 130 (right): Courtesy of Rawganique
p. 131 (left): Courtesy of VivaTerra
p. 131 (right): Courtesy of Allergy Buyers Club

p. 132 (left): © Liza mcCorkle/shutterstock
p. 132 (right): Courtesy of White Lotus Home
p. 133 (left): Courtesy of Natural Collection
p. 133 (right): Courtesy of Phoenix Organics
p. 134 (left): Courtesy of The Company Store
p. 134 (right): Courtesy of H3 Environmental, The Mary Cordaro Collection
p. 135 (left): © Naomi Hasegawa/ istockphoto
p. 135 (right): Courtesy of H3 Environmental, The Mary Cordaro Collection
p. 136 (left): Courtesy of Coyuchi
p. 136 (right): Courtesy of O~Wool
p. 137 (left): Courtesy of Dream Sack
p. 137 (right): Courtesy of Dream Sack
p. 138 (left): Courtesy of The Company Store
p. 138 (right): Courtesy of Good Night Naturals
p. 139 (left): Courtesy of The Company Store
p. 140 (left): Courtesy of Home Source International
p. 140 (right): Courtesy of VivaTerra
p. 141 (left): Provided by High Desert Naturals, Inc. © Chris Mather/Dog Leg Studios
p. 141 (right): Courtesy of The Company Store

Chapter 13
p. 142 (left): Courtesy of Kohler Co.
p. 142 (right): Dolzura Cararra Marble Sink by SinksGallery.com
p. 143 (left): Alabaster Swirl Glass Vessel Sink by SinksGallery.com
p. 143 (right): Courtesy of Stone Forest
p. 144 (left): Courtesy of American Standard
p. 144 (right): Courtesy of Kohler Co.
p. 145 (left): Courtesy of Kohler Co.
p. 146 (left): Courtesy of Kohler Co.
p. 146 (right): Courtesy of Kohler Co.
p. 147 (left): Courtesy of Stone Soup Concrete
p. 147 (right): Courtesy of Fine Crafts & Imports
p. 148 (left): Courtesy of Oxygenics
p. 148 (right): © Marek Tihelka/istockphoto
p. 149 (left): Courtesy of Wellness Enterprises
p. 149 (right): Courtesy of Danze
p. 150 (left): Courtesy of TOTO USA, INC

p. 150 (right): © Tomo Jesenecnik/ shutterstock
p. 152 (left): © Marc Dietrich/shutterstock
p. 152 (right): © Graca Victoria/shutterstock
p. 153 (left): © Tatiana Popovo/shutterstock
p. 153 (right): © Jim Jurica/istockphoto

Chapter 14
p. 154 (left): Courtesy of Vivavi Inc.
p. 154 (right): Courtesy of A Natural Home
p. 155 (left): Courtesy of Little Merry Fellows
p. 155 (right): Courtesy of Celery Furniture
p. 156 (left): Courtesy of Nursery Works
p. 156 (right): Courtesy of Coyuchi
p. 157 (left): Courtesy of Nursery Works
p. 157 (right): Courtesy of H3 Environmental, The Mary Cordaro Collection
p. 158 (left): Courtesy of Nursery Works
p. 158 (right): Courtesy of Gary Weeks
p. 159 (left): Courtesy of Everything Best Baby
p. 159 (right): © Steve Bromberg Photography 2008
p. 160 (left): © Christy Thompson/ istockphoto
p. 160 (right): Courtesy of The Old Fashioned Milk Paint Co., Inc.
p. 161 (left): © Marilyn Nieves/istockphoto
p. 161 (right): Courtesy of Smith and Noble
p. 162 (left): (c) Brian McEntire/istockphoto
p. 162 (right): Courtesy of Eco Timber
p. 163 (left): Courtesy of Allergy Buyers Club
p. 163 (right): Courtesy of Flor
p. 164 (left): Courtesy of Luna Lullaby
p. 164 (right): Courtesy of Coyuchi
p. 165 (left): © Tim Kimberley/istockphoto
p. 165 (right): © DK images

Chapter 15
p. 166 (left): Courtesy of Y Lighting
p. 166 (right): Courtesy of Y Lighting
p. 167 (left): Courtesy of Shop Blue House
p. 167 (right): Courtesy of BranchHome.com
p. 168 (left): Courtesy of Knoend
p. 168 (right): Courtesy of Natural Collection
p. 169 (left): Courtesy of Lamponi's Lamps
p. 169 (right): Courtesy of VivaTerra
p. 170 (left): Courtesy of Y Lighting
p. 170 (right): Courtesy of Vivavi
p. 171 (left): Courtesy of Re-Modern

p. 171 (right): Courtesy of W.A.C. Lighting
p. 172 (left): Courtesy of Vessl Inc.
p. 172 (right): Coutesy of AcaciaCatalog.com
p. 173 (left): Courtesy of Green Light Concepts
p. 173 (right): Courtesy of Chopstick Art
p. 174 (left): Courtesy of Bulbs.com
p. 174 (right): Courtesy of Bulbs.com
p. 175 (left): Courtesy of Bulbs.com
p. 175 (right): Courtesy of Bulbs.com
p. 176 (left): Courtesy of Y Lighting
p. 176 (right): Courtesy of Y Lighting
p. 177 (left): Courtesy of Smart Home
p. 177 (right): Courtesy of Power Cost Monitor

Chapter 16
p. 178 (left): Courtesy of AcaciaCatalog.com
p. 178 (right): Courtesy of Michael Aram, Inc.
p. 179 (left): Courtesy of BranchHome.com
p. 179 (right): Courtesy of OrganicBouquet.com
p. 180 (left): Courtesy of VivaTerra
p. 180 (right): Courtesy of VivaTerra
p. 181 (left): Courtesy of Eco-Artware.com
p. 181 (right): Courtesy of VivaTerra
p. 182 (left): Courtesy of Eco-Artware.com
p. 182 (right): Courtesy of VivaTerra
p. 183 (left): Courtesy of Good Humans
p. 183 (right): Courtesy of Vivavi
p. 184 (left): Courtesy of Gaiam
p. 184 (right): Courtesy of Spectra Décor
p. 185 (left): © rebvt/shutterstock
p. 185 (right): Courtesy of Vivavi
p. 186 (left): Courtesy of Rawganique
p. 186 (right): Courtesy of Gaiam
p. 187 (left): Courtesy of Chefs Catalogue
p. 187 (right): Courtesy of Gaiam
p. 188 (left): Courtesy of Eco-Artware.com
p. 188 (right): Courtesy of Design Public
p. 189 (left): Courtesy of Haba
p. 189 (right): Courtesy of The Powell Company

Chapter 17
p. 190 (left): Courtesy of BellaDogga.com
p. 190 (right): Courtesy of Only Natural Pet

p. 191 (left): Courtesy of A Natural Home
p. 191 (right): Courtesy of BranchHome.com
p. 192 (left): Courtesy of BellaDogga.com
p. 192 (right): Courtesy of Big Dog Boutique
p. 193 (left): Courtesy of Annie's Sweat Shop
p. 194 (left): Courtesy of George
p. 194 (right): Courtesy of EcoAnimal
p. 195 (left): Courtesy of Organic Style Ltd.
p. 195 (right): Courtesy of Planet Dog
p. 196 (left): © Bojan Pavlukovic/shutterstock
p. 196 (right): Courtesy of George
p. 197 (left): Courtesy of Vivavi
p. 197 (right): Courtesy of Ergo Systems Inc
p. 198 (left): Courtesy of Far Fetched Inc.
p. 198 (right): Courtesy of Cuddle Down
p. 199 (left): Courtesy of Red Dog House
p. 199 (right): Courtesy of Cat's Rule
p. 200 (left): © iofoto/shutterstock
p. 201 (left): © Vicki Stephensen/istockphoto

Chapter 18
p. 202 (left): Courtesy of Custom Rustic Furniture
p. 202 (right): Courtesy of Lloyd/Flanders Inc.
p. 203 (left): Courtesy of Bamboo Hardwoods
p. 203 (right): Courtesy of Spirit Elements
p. 204 (left): Courtesy of Rustic Cedar
p. 204 (right): Courtesy of Greenfeet
p. 205 (left): Courtesy of Cabinfield
p. 205 (right): Courtesy of Thos. Baker LLC
p. 206 (left): Courtesy of Design Public
p. 206 (right): Courtesy of O.W. Lee
p. 207 (left): Courtesy of VivaTerra
p. 207 (right): Courtesy of Green Culture
p. 208 (left): Courtesy of Natural Area Rugs
p. 208 (right): Courtesy of Sundance Catalog
p. 209 (right): Courtesy of VivaTerra
p. 210 (left): Courtesy of Organic Style Ltd.
p. 210 (right): Courtesy of Gardeners Supply Company
p. 211 (left): Courtesy of Kichler Lighting
p. 211 (right): Courtesy of Green Culture
p. 212 (left): Courtesy of Greener Grass Design

p. 212 (right): Courtesy of Recycled Products
p. 213 (left): Courtesy of VivaTerra
p. 213 (right): Courtesy of Gaiam

Chapter 19
p. 214 (left): Courtesy of American Iron and Steel Institute (AISI)
p. 214 (right): © Alison Gannett
p. 215 (left): Courtesy of Eco Timber
p. 215 (right): Courtesy of Columbia Forest Products
p. 216 (left): Courtesy of The Forest Stewardship Council
p. 216 (right): Courtesy of Bamboo Revolution
p. 217 (left): Courtesy of Humabuilt
p. 217 (right): Courtesy of TerraMai
p. 218 (left): Courtesy of Andersen Windows and Doors
p. 218 (right): Courtesy of Andersen Windows and Doors
p. 219 (left): Courtesy of Andersen Windows and Doors
p. 219 (right): © Arda Guldogan/istockphoto
p. 220 (left): © Andrew Hyslop/istockphoto
p. 220 (right): Courtesy of Ludowici Roof Tile
p. 221 (left): Courtesy of Cedar Shake & Shingle Bureau
p. 221 (right): Courtesy of EcoStar, a division of Carlisle SynTec
p. 222 (left): Courtesy of Advantage Trim & Lumber Co.
p. 222 (right): Courtesy of TerraMai
p. 223 (left): © photoBeard/shutterstock
p. 223 (right): Courtesy of the Western Red Cedar Lumber Associatio
p. 224 (left): Courtesy of RainChains.com
p. 224 (right): Courtesy of Stacks and Stacks
p. 225 (left): Courtesy of Rain Harvesting
p. 225 (right): © Suzanne Carter-Jackson/istockphoto

INDEX

INDEX

INDEX